CAMBRIDGE
UNIVERSITY PRESS

CAMBRIDGE
Primary English

Learner's Book 1

Gill Budgell

CAMBRIDGE
UNIVERSITY PRESS

University Printing House, Cambridge CB2 8BS, United Kingdom

One Liberty Plaza, 20th Floor, New York, NY 10006, USA

477 Williamstown Road, Port Melbourne, VIC 3207, Australia

314–321, 3rd Floor, Plot 3, Splendor Forum, Jasola District Centre,
New Delhi – 110025, India

103 Penang Road, #05–06/07, Visioncrest Commercial, Singapore 238467

Cambridge University Press is part of the University of Cambridge.

It furthers the University's mission by disseminating knowledge in the pursuit of
education, learning and research at the highest international levels of excellence.

www.cambridge.org
Information on this title: www.cambridge.org/9781108749879

© Cambridge University Press 2021

First published 2015
Second edition 2021

20 19 18 17 16 15 14 13 12 11 10 9 8 7 6 5 4 3 2 1

Printed in Malaysia by Vivar Printing

A catalogue record for this publication is available from the British Library

ISBN 978-1-108-74987-9 Paperback with Digital Access (1 Year)
ISBN 978-1-108-96405-0 Digital Learner's Book 1
ISBN 978-1-108-96406-7 Learner's Book 1 – eBook

Additional resources for this publication at www.cambridge.org/go

Introduction

Welcome to Stage 1 of Cambridge Primary English.

This book will help you to learn how to speak, listen, read and write English better.

There are nine units.

Three units are fiction.

Three units are non-fiction.

Three units are rhymes and poetry.

In the units you will:

- talk about new ideas and learn new words

- listen to others and share what you already know

- read and write

- work with the class, in a group, with a partner or on your own.

- act, sing, make things and play fun language games

- look back to talk about your learning.

Look for me and my friends in the book for top tips and help.

At the end of each unit, there are ideas for projects that you can do on your own, with a partner, or as a group or class.

I hope you enjoy the stories, information texts and poems I have chosen for you. Have fun in Cambridge Primary English Stage 1.

Gill Budgell

Contents

Speaking/Listening	Language focus	Cross-curricular links	21st century skills
Retell a story using a story map and puppets Listen to a rhyming story Ask a book character questions Act a story using mask	Using and Compound words	Maths: telling the time; fractions; block graphs and pictograms; 2D shapes Science: exploring materials; sound; animal survival; stars; similarities and differences Geography: different landscapes; map features Art: modelling and painting love bowls	Using critical thinking to make predictions about what happens next in a story Act parts of a story in a group, using actions and body language creatively
Listen carefully to find information Retell a diary using pictures Retell a recount using actions Listen for –s and –es plurals Tip: Using the past tense in speech Tip: Practising letter sounds Tip: Using a loud clear voice Tip: Using a sentence frame Tip: How to listen carefully	Using and Plural noun endings	Maths: counting in 2s and 3s; writing numerals; exploring local currency; exploring time Science: rainbows Art: creating finger puppets; mixing colours; language of colour Music: exploring rhythm	Reflect on ways to remember the alphabet Use critical thinking to answer questions about diaries
Perform an action rhyme Work in pairs to say rhymes with actions Act a nonsense rhyme Listen for rhythm in a story Share poetry writing Tip: Ways to listen well	Linking rhyme to spelling	Maths: fractions; 2D shapes; block graphs and pictograms; counting; sorting into sets; language of length; shape patterns Science: parts of plants; living things; materials; movement of objects; rainbows Art: making puppets; pancake models and paintings; paintings of trees and flowers Music: exploring rhythm	Reflect on how pictures can help with reading Work creatively to write a poem about colours
Retell a story in groups with masks Talk about story endings Listen carefully to answer questions Join in with a story in groups Act a story in a group Tip: Taking turns to speak	Capital letters and full stops Using and Using the, a and an Plurals	Maths: symbols; 2D shapes; fractions; capacity Science: making predictions; tools and equipment; senses Art: capital letter patterns; mixing colours PSED: alternative communication Music: colour songs	Make a character mask and use it to act a story in a group Use critical thinking to make predictions about characters in a story

Contents

Speaking/Listening	Language focus	Cross-curricular links	21st century skills
Talk about and describe signs Act the meaning of a sign Listen carefully to follow a text Talk about instructional posters Tip: How to speak well Tip: Listening to numbers in instructions Tip: Listening to others	Full stops	Maths: symbols and codes in maths; measuring time PSED: research methods of communicating without words Science: adjectives and connectives in science, explanation texts in experiments; using drones to collect information; giving and receiving instructions	Present a sign design to the class Work with a partner to follow origami instructions
Play a game of I spy … I hear Listen carefully to answer questions Perform a poem in a group Listen to a poem and give feedback Tips: Ways to perform well	Verb endings	Maths: block charts and pictograms Science: asking questions Art: word pictures; sand pictures; punctuation pictures Technology: exploring animal sound files	Work collaboratively to create a class A–Z of feelings Work with a partner to check work
Listen carefully to answer questions Listen to follow a text Act a story Retell a story	Using a, an and the	Maths: sides of shapes Science: local plants; stars; animal survival; making predictions; exploring slime; sorting and grouping objects Geography: countries; different environments Art: star patterns; artistic lettering Music: exploring music about stars	Create a map of a pretend land in a group Work creatively to write a pretend scary story
Describe an animal Listen to match information with pictures Play a game to recall the alphabet	Using and and because Common words	Maths: charts Science: grouping living things; similarities and differences in humans All: exploring book covers, contents pages, photos and illustrations	Use communication skills to describe an animal to a partner Reflect on preferred ways of finding information.
Say or sing a poem aloud Listen carefully to recall information Listen to a poem to help with imagination Tip: Ways to speak and sing well	Using and Capital letters and full stops	Science: the sun as a star; plant survival; melting; pushes and pulls; Geography: differet landscapes Art: shape poems; ice scuptures; weather paintings Technology: storm sounds Music: weather music	Work creatively to write a shape poem Discuss questions in a group

How to use this book

In this book you will find lots of different features to help your learning.

Questions to find out what you know already. ⟶

> **Getting started**
> With a partner, remember and talk about a favourite experience.
> 1 What kind of experience was it?
> 2 When was it?
> 3 Who were you with?

What you will learn in ⟶ the unit.

> **We are going to...**
> • listen to and read a story about helping at home.

Fun activities linked to what you are learning. ⟶

> 1 Work in pairs. Answer the questions to plan your story.
>   a Who is your main character?
>   b What other characters will you have? Choose up to four.
>   c What is the problem? Did you lose something?
>   d How is the problem fixed? Did you find it?

Important words to learn. ⟶

> **Key word**
> narrator: the story teller.

Key language and grammar rules explained. ⟶

> **Language focus**
> We can use **and** to join words and sentences together.
> Hide **and** Seek
> She liked to fill up their dish **and** watch them peck.

Questions to help you ⟶ think about how you learn.

> What helped you most: reading quietly to yourself or reading out loud? Why?

Hints to help you with your reading, writing, speaking and listening skills. →

Speaking tip

When we are telling someone about an experience we use the past tense. We use the past tense to 'recount' the experience.

This is what you have learned in the unit. ——→

Look what I can do!

☐ I can explore different ways to tell people about things that have happened in the past.

☐ I can retell information from a recount.

☐ I can read recounts and answer questions.

☐ I can make an A–Z chart and say the days of the week.

☐ I can plan and write a postcard.

☐ I can check my writing and talk about my learning in the unit.

Questions that cover what you have learned in the unit. If you can answer these, you are ready to move on to the next unit. ——→

Check your progress

Answer the questions below to show what you have learned in this unit.

1 What is a recount?

2 Which word tells you when this happened?
Yesterday I went on a train ride.

3 Say or sing the alphabet.

4 Finish the sequence: Monday, Tuesday ...

5 Join these two sentences together. Jared swims every day.
Next week he is going to try body surfing!

Projects for you to carry out, using what you have learned. You might make something or solve a problem. ——→

Projects

Group project: Set up a class post office. Find or make all the things you need to go in it. For example, you might need some stamps and some envelopes or a sign to say your post office is open.

Pair project: Make an envelope by folding paper.
Write a letter to go inside.

Solo Project: For two weeks, write or draw something in a diary about what you have done each day.
Do you like writing a diary? You may decide to carry on!

A good time to pause and find out how your learning is progressing. ——→

How are we doing?

Look in a reading book. See how many common words like went, to, walked, the, was and my you can find and read in 1 minute.

Ask someone to time you.

1 ▶ Places we know

❯ 1.1 At home

We are going to...

- listen to a story set at home, finding information in the pictures.

Getting started

Talk about the pictures.

1 Which places do you know?

2 Which places do you *not* know?

3 What other places do you know?

1 Read this sentence.

It was Jamal's birthday.

What else does the picture tell you?

Where is Jamal?

What time is it?

Why is he awake?

What can you see?

It's about a special morning at home.

2 Listen to *It's Much Too Early!* by Ian Whybrow.

Point to each picture as you listen.

It's Much Too Early!

At five o'clock, Jamal got out of bed and looked at the presents.
'Hooray!' said Jamal.
'It's a scooter!'

He went into Mum and Dad's room.
'Go back to bed, Jamal!
It's much too early!'

At six o'clock, he went into
Malik's room.
'Go back to bed, Jamal!
It's much too early!'

At seven o'clock, Jamal took his
new scooter downstairs.
'Look out,' he said to the cat.
The cat jumped onto the table.
Oh, no!

Mum came downstairs.
'I wanted to ride my new scooter,'
Jamal said.
'But it's much too early,' Mum said.
'It's only 7 o'clock.'

At eight o'clock, it was time
to get up.
'Where is Jamal?' said Malik.

'Happy Birthday, Jamal!' said Mum,
Dad and Malik.
'I want to sleep,' said Jamal.
'It's much too early!'

Ian Whybrow

Did you guess from the picture in question 1 that the present was a scooter? How?

3 a Talk about what Jamal did each time he got up.

b Talk about what you do at home in the morning.

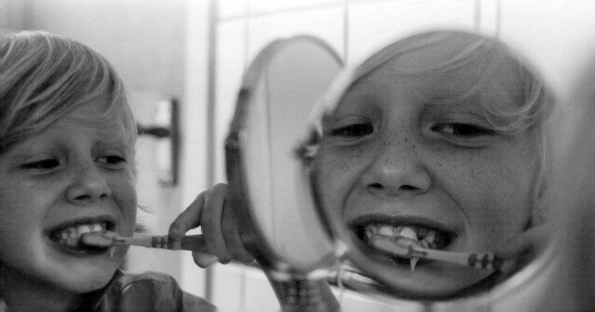

⟩ 1.2 Retelling

We are going to...

- **retell a story using pictures.**

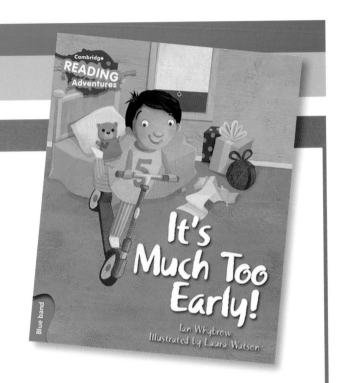

Getting started

Look at this book cover.

Talk about these questions with a partner.

1 What is the title of the story?

2 How many capital letters can you see in the title?

3 What else can you see on the book cover?

1 Read *It's Much Too Early!* together.
Write answers to these questions in your notebook.

a How many times can you find these words and sentences?

Go back to bed, Jamal!

It's much too early!

At _____ o'clock...

How are we doing?

What can you do to help find the words in the text?

b Who says these words?

2 Sort the pictures into the correct order. Use them to retell the story. Write your answers in your notebook.

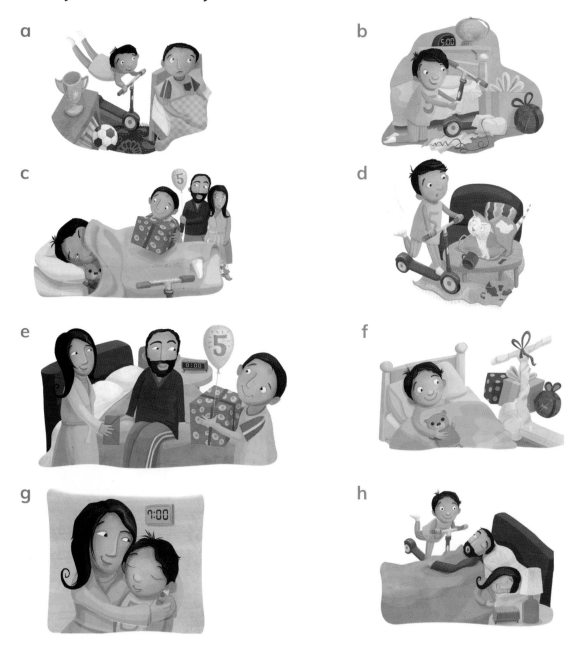

a

b

c

d

e

f

g

h

I remember how the story started: *At five o'clock, Jamal got out of bed …*

3 a Draw Jamal's red scooter in your notebook.

b Write sentences about the scooter using 'It's much too _____'. You can use these words to help you.

big

heavy

noisy

new

It's much too shiny!

It's much too heavy to lift.

> 1.3 Helping at home

We are going to...

- **listen to and read a story about helping at home.**

Getting started

What are these children doing to help at home?

How do you help at home?

1 **a** Listen to and read part 1 of *Don't Spill the Milk!*

Point to each picture as you listen.

Don't Spill the Milk!, Part 1

1 Penda lived in a tiny village in Africa.
'Let me go to the **grasslands** to take Daddy his milk. Please, please, please!'
'All right,' said her mum, 'but try very hard not to spill any milk on the way.'

2 Penda picked a path over the downy **dunes**.
Don't slip, don't slide, girl, don't fall over.
Don't let a single droplet drop on the sand.

3 Penda didn't stop to look at the masked dancers.
Walk tall, walk steady, eyes on the horizon, girl. Don't even think about spilling any milk.

4 Penda took a ride across the river in a stinky fishing boat.
Don't shiver, don't quiver, don't fall in the river, girl.
Keep it on your head, girl, milk don't float.

Glossary

grassland: a big area of land covered in grass

dunes: hills made of sand

5 Penda didn't stop to look at the white giraffes.
Don't look, don't turn your head, just walk on through. You're not at the zoo, girl, you've got work to do.

6 Penda breathed in deep and up she climbed one final mountain.
Left foot, right foot, never give up, girl.
Left hand, right hand, all the way up now.
At last Penda arrived at the grasslands!

Christopher Corr

b Listen again. Point to the words and join in when you can.

How are we doing?

What do you say to encourage yourself not to give up?

2 Read the sentences. Say true or false.

a Penda carries the milk in a bowl.

b Penda went over the dunes.

c Penda swam across the river.

3 Say what you think happens when Penda gets to the grasslands.

> 1.4 Joining in

We are going to...

- **listen and join in with repeated parts of a story.**

Getting started

What do you remember about Penda's journey?
Work with a partner.

1 Where did she go?

2 What did she see?

3 Draw each thing in the right order.

Only look back in the book when you have tried to remember!

1 a Listen to and read part 2 of *Don't Spill the Milk!*

b Listen again. Point to the words and join in where you can.

Don't Spill the Milk!, Part 2

1 At last Penda arrived at the grasslands!

'Hi, Daddy. I've brought you some milk,' said Penda.

'Hi, Penda. Nice to see you.'

She took the bowl off her head, but just as she was passing it to Daddy …

2 A big fat mango landed right in the bowl! Daddy's milk spilt everywhere.

'I don't believe it!' wailed Penda. 'I carried that milk over the dunes, across the river and up the mountains and I didn't stop to look at the masked dancers or the white giraffes, because I didn't want to spill a single drop and now look – IT'S ALL GONE!'

3 Daddy gave Penda a big hug.

'It's not all gone,' he whispered. 'There was more than milk in that bowl. Your love for me was in that bowl as well.'

'Huh?' said Penda.

4 'You carried it over the dunes, across the river and up the mountain and you didn't stop to look at the masked dancers or the white giraffes. You brought it all the way up to the grasslands and you gave it to me just fine. That bowl was full of love, girl, and it still is. You didn't spill a drop.'

Christopher Corr

2 Read the questions. Write the answers in your notebook.

  a What did Penda see when she got to the grasslands?

  b Where was Daddy sitting?

  c What fell in the bowl?

3 Read these words. Find them in the story.

milk   just   spilt   stop   drop

> 1.5 Story maps and retelling

We are going to...

- retell a story using a story map and puppets.

Getting started

Talk about this story map. What story does it tell?

1 Look at the pictures on the next page.

Sort the pictures by letter into the correct order.

Draw something from each picture to make a story map to retell the story.

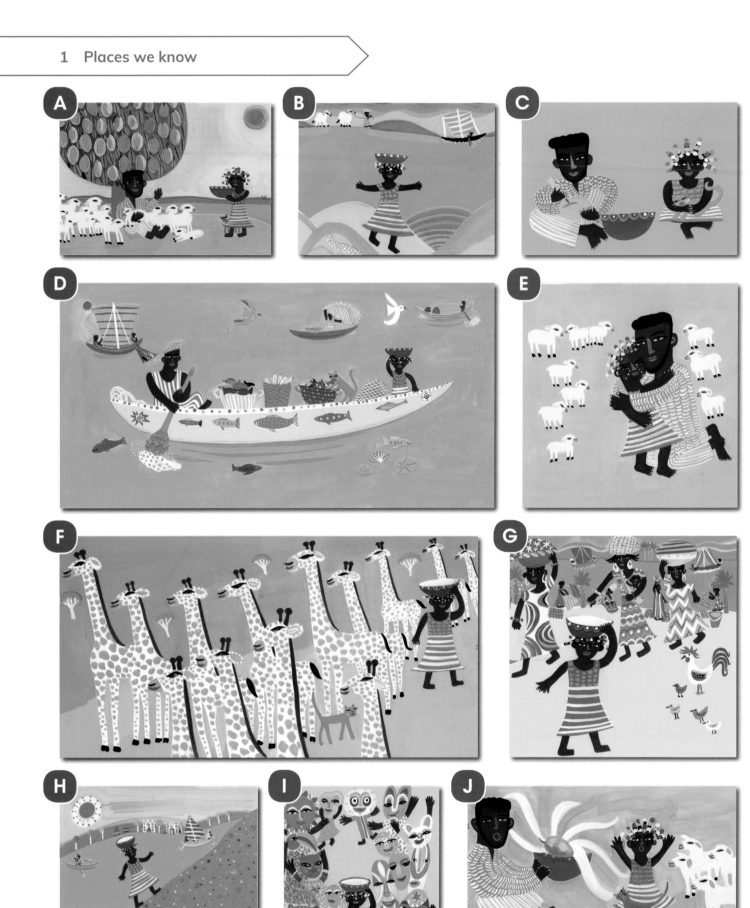

2 Retell the story using your story map.

Say one or two sentences for each of your pictures.

3 a Make puppets.

You will need puppets for:

b Retell the story using your story map and puppets.

〉 1.6 At school

We are going to…

- **read a story set in a classroom.**

Getting started

Some classrooms are outside.   Some classrooms are inside.

Continued

Talk to a partner.

1   What is your school like?

2   Where is your classroom?

3   What is your classroom like?

Reading tip

If you get stuck on a word, sound its letter sounds out loud.

1   Read *Hide and Seek* by Lynne Rickards.

Hide and Seek

Zara liked feeding the baby chicks.
She liked to fill up their dish and watch them peck.
'One, two, three chicks,' said Zara. 'Fluff, Puff and Scruff.'

One day the cage door was open and Zara looked inside.
One, two ... wait! Where was Scruff?
'Miss Garcia!' called Zara. 'Scruff is gone! We have to find her!'

All the children jumped up to help.
Omar and Benu looked on the floor.
Zara and Leila looked on shelves and tables.
Kofi looked under Miss Garcia's desk.

'Shh, class!' said Miss Garcia. 'I can hear a noise.
Let's listen.' All the children stood still. *Scratch, scratch.*
There **was** a noise! The scratching was coming from the cage!

Scratch, scratch, scratch ... peep, peep, peep!
'There she is!' said Miss Garcia. 'She was in the cage all the time.'
'I think Scruff was playing Hide and Seek!' said Zara.

Lynne Rickards

Had Scruff run back into the cage? Or was she there all the time?

2   Match the questions to the correct answers.

Question	Answer
a Who likes feeding the chicks?	**1** The cage door was open.
b What does Zara fill up the chick's dish with?	**2** Zara.
c What are the chicks called?	**3** With chick food like seeds.
d What happened one day?	**4** They followed the *scratch* and *peep* sounds back to the cage.
e What did the children do?	**5** Fluff, Puff and Scruff.
f How did they find Scruff?	**6** They looked on and under things in the classroom.

Language focus

We can use **and** to join words and sentences together.

Hide **and** *Seek*

She liked to fill up their dish **and** *watch them peck.*

3   Add *and* to say these words and sentences together.

Write them in your notebook. Draw a picture for each.

	and	
Miss Garcia looked in the cage		Kofi looked under a desk.
Fluff, Puff		watch them peck.
Beno looked on the floor		seek.
She liked to fill up their dish		Scruff.
Hide		she found Scruff.

> 1.7 Changing and retelling

We are going to...

• change a story and retell it.

Getting started

Let's pretend! If you could choose to have animals in your classroom, what would you choose? Why?

Use these ideas to help you.

1   Retell the story using the pictures.

Title: Hide and Seek

a

b

c

d

e

f

2   Write a sentence for each picture in your notebook.

Use these words to help you.

| Characters: **Zara** | **chicks** |
| **Fluff, Puff and Scruff** | **Miss Garcia** |

| Setting: **classroom** |

Places they looked: **in the cage**	**on the floor**
on the shelves	**on the tables**
under the desk	

| Noises: **scratch** | **peep** |

Key words

characters: the people or animals in a story.

setting: where a story happens.

3 With a partner, change the story so it is about different class pets.

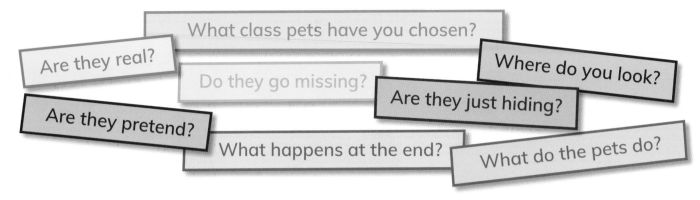

What class pets have you chosen?

Are they real?

Do they go missing?

Where do you look?

Are they just hiding?

Are they pretend?

What happens at the end?

What do the pets do?

How are we doing?

Tell your new story to others. What do they think?

> ## 1.8 When things we know look different

We are going to...

• **listen and ask questions about a story to work out its meaning.**

Getting started

Talk about the ways these things look.

1 What are they?

2 What do they look like?

Sometimes things we know can look different!

 1 Listen to *The Park in the Dark* by Martin Waddell. It is a rhyming story.

    a Draw what you think 'the THING' is.

    b Show your drawing to a partner. Did they draw the same thing?

2 Listen again.

    a What questions do you want to ask the story characters about their adventure?

    b Write some questions. Work in pairs.

Writing tip

Remember to begin your question with a capital letter.

How did you feel at first in the park?

Why are you going out so late and alone?

3 Listen again. Act these parts of the story in groups of three.

> How can you use your body to show how you feel?

Softly down the staircase ... trying to look small ...

It's shivery out in the dark on our way to the park ...

WHOOPEE!

4 Draw something that can look different.

a Draw what it really is.

b Then draw how it can look!

c Write a sentence for your pictures.

Coats can look like ...

... a monster bear!

> 1.9 Out and about

We are going to...

- listen to and read a story that is set out and about.

Getting started

1 Look at these pictures. How many differences can you see?

2 What do you notice?

How are we doing?

What helps you to look really carefully?

1 Listen to this part of *Finders keepers*.

Point to the words and pictures as you listen.

Finders keepers Part 1

2 Read the story with a partner and answer the questions.

   a Where is this story set?

   b In this story Ashraf does not notice something. What is it?

Language focus

Sometimes we can join two words to make one word.

no	where
some	body
any	way
	thing

3   Look for these words in the story.

anywhere   something   nobody

a   Make a note to show how many times you find each of the words.

b   Say:

  Nobody has seen Ashraf's scarf.

4   Choose one person to be Fox. Think of questions to ask Fox about why he did not tell the truth.

What would your mummy say?

Why did you… ?

How did it make you feel when… ?

› 1.10 Story endings

We are going to...

- **talk about story endings and read one.**

Getting started

Play a game: Back to back

1 Sit back to back with a partner.

2 Player one describes a picture.

3 Player two draws the picture.

4 Use these pictures to help you.

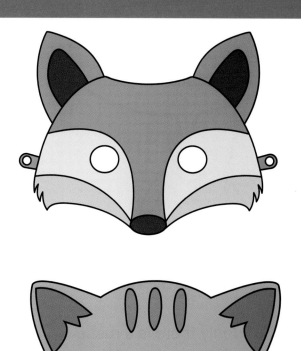

5 Compare the two pictures. Are they the same? Why?

6 Swap and play again.

1   Cover the pictures. Say how you think the story will end.

Together, read this part of the story to find out how it ends.

Finder keepers – Part 2

1 Ashraf meets Owl.

You look sad, Ashraf. What are you looking for?

2 Ashraf tells Owl about his scarf.

I lost my scarf in the woods. It must be here but nobody has seen it. I need to look more carefully.

3 Suddenly there is a rustle in the woods. Ashraf sees something long, warm and brightly coloured flash through the trees.
It's his scarf! It's Fox!

4 What do you think Ashraf says to Fox?

I found it in the woods so I kept it – finders keepers! I didn't know it was yours. I tied it to my tail and I thought it looked nice.

2 Say what you think about the characters.

Ashraf is kind.

Owl is helpful.

Ashraf should share.

Fox likes to play tricks.

Imagine you want Ashraf's scarf. Would you take it without asking?

3 Make masks and make a brightly coloured scarf.

Work in a group to act the story.

> 1.11 Planning and writing

We are going to...

- plan and write a story like one we know.

Getting started

Talk about the story features in *Finders keepers*.

A main character

Key word

story features: things we find in a story.

Other characters

A problem

1   Work in pairs. Answer the questions to plan your story.

   a   Who is your main character?

   b   What other characters will you have? Choose up to four.

   c   What is the problem? Did you lose something?

   d   How is the problem fixed? Did you find it?

2   Use your ideas from Activity 1 to write your story.

Write your sentences into your notebook.
Draw some pictures for each section.

3   Write your story in a
zig-zag book.

> 1.12 Look back

We are going to...

- **check our writing and talk about all the unit stories.**

Getting started

Together, find out more about story books that are:

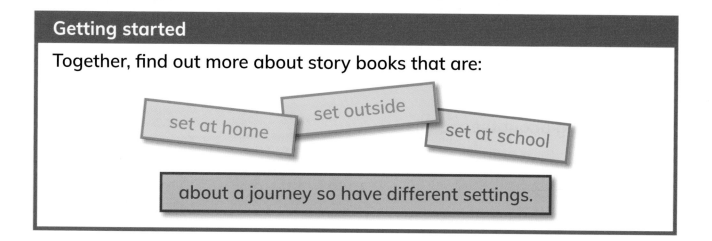

set at home

set outside

set at school

about a journey so have different settings.

1 Check your writing from Session 1.11.

   a Find one spelling mistake.

   b Find one word you can write better.

   c Read your new story.

Did you remember to write a title for your new story?

How are we doing?

Share your story and see what others think.

2 Look back at all the stories in this unit.

   a Talk about them with a partner.

   b Try to remember the characters and the settings.

3 Sing a song about these skills.

reading   writing   spelling   listening   speaking

Look what I can do!

- ☐ I can explore different story settings.
- ☐ I can listen to stories, finding information in the pictures.
- ☐ I can join in with and retell stories using story maps and puppets.
- ☐ I can read stories and answer questions.
- ☐ I can plan to change and write a story.
- ☐ I can check my writing and talk about all the stories in the unit.

Check your progress

Answer the questions below to show what you have learned in this unit.

1 What is a story setting?
2 Which are the rhyming words: Don't shiver, don't quiver, don't fall in the river, girl.
3 What does a book cover usually tell you?
4 In The Park in the Dark: What was real? What was pretend?
5 Write another word spelled like:
    a Hide with i_e
    b Seek with ee
6 Finish the sentence: The best story in this unit was …

Projects

Group project: Make a class A–Z of story settings.

Pair project: Design and make a simple map of Penda's journey.

Solo Project: Individually, make a painting or models of Fluff, Puff and Scruff from Hide and Seek.

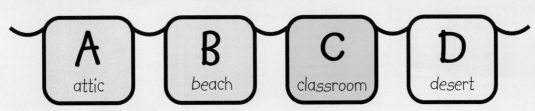

2 > Let me tell you!

> 2.1 First experiences

We are going to...

- **talk about, listen to and read about doing things for the first time.**

Getting started

Talk about the photos.

1 What are the children doing for the first time?

2 What do you remember doing for the first time?

1 With a partner, look at the front and back cover of this book.

   a Name the parts of the book.

   b Ask and answer these questions with a partner.

   • Which is the back cover?

   • Which is the front cover?

   • Where is the title?

   • What is the author's name?

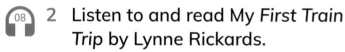

2 Listen to and read My *First Train Trip* by Lynne Rickards.

   Point to each picture as you listen.

It's about going on a train for the first time.

My First Train Trip

Yesterday I went on a train ride.
The station was very big.
Lots of people were travelling on trains.

Why do you think I was going on a train?
We went to the ticket office to buy our tickets. The ticket seller told us to go to Platform 5.

We waited on the platform for our train.

We got on when it arrived. We found some free seats. I sat by the window and looked out.

The train was very slow as it went through the city.
At first, I saw streets and buildings. Some people waved.

Then I saw fields and trees. Some people were working in the fields.

It was a long train trip. At last I saw streets and buildings again. We were nearly there and the train was slowing down.

Grandpa was waiting for us on the platform. It was a great first train trip!

Lynne Rickards

Did you guess the girl was visiting somebody? How?

3   Read these sentences. Now say them as if you went yesterday.

   a Today I am going on a train ride. *Yesterday I went on a train ride.*

   b The station is big.

   c We get a ticket.

   d We find our seat.

   e The train is slow.

   f It is a long train trip.

   g Grandpa is on the platform.

Speaking tip

When we are telling someone about an experience we use the past tense. We use the past tense to 'recount' the experience.

4   Find words in the text that begin with two consonants.
   Copy them to make a list.

Speaking tip

The word *train* begins with letters *tr* and so does the word *trip*!
Say the sounds in each word:

t-r-ai-n   t-r-i-p

> 2.2 Retelling with pictures

We are going to...

- **retell a recount of a first experience using pictures.**

Getting started

With a partner, remember and talk about a favourite experience.

1 What kind of experience was it?

2 When was it?

3 Who were you with?

1 Together as a class, read *My First Train Trip* again.

Put up your hand when you hear or read something to do with a train station.

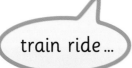

train ride...

station

trains

2 Answer the questions about *My First Train Trip*.

Where was I yesterday?

What was the station like?

What did we do first?

Who was on the platform when we arrived?

Why did I sit near a window?

Where did we wait for the train?

3 Sort the pictures into the correct order.

Use them to retell the story.

Use the words in Activity 1 to help you.

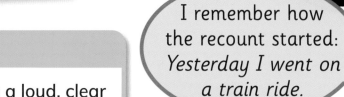

I remember how the recount started: *Yesterday I went on a train ride.*

Speaking tip

Make sure you use a loud, clear voice when you are retelling the story. Don't rush!

⟩ 2.3 I remember ...

We are going to...

- **talk about, remember and write about a first experience.**

Getting started

Listen to these children talking about their first day at school.

1 Listen for one thing the boy remembers.

2 Listen for one thing the girl remembers.

What do you remember about your first day at school?

1 Say the alphabet or sing an alphabet song.

How are we doing?

How else can you remember the English alphabet?

2 Make an A–Z of first experiences you remember.

Work in a group.

Draw or write your ideas like this.

I remember the first time…		Aa I picked apples from the tree.	Bb A bee stung me.
Cc	Dd	Ee	Ff
Gg	Hh	Ii	Jj
Kk	Ll	Mm A monkey sat on my head.	Nn
Oo	Pp	Qq	Rr
Ss I went on a swing.	Tt	Uu	Vv
Ww	Xx I had an x-ray!	Yy	Zz

3 Choose a first experience from the A–Z that you want to write about.

a Use these ideas to help you.

I remember the first time I …

I felt …

b Say, draw and write three things you remember about it.

> 2.4 What's in a week?

We are going to...

- **listen to, talk and read about personal experiences in a diary.**

Getting started

Sing a days of the week song!

1 Point to each day of the week and sing it out loud.

2 Say what day it is today.

3 What day was it yesterday?

1 Listen to and read this diary.

Date _/_/_ Week 14

Monday	I travelled to the library on a bus. It was a reading day.
Tuesday	I skated to town on my roller skates. It was a shopping day.
Wednesday	I went to Dad's restaurant in his car. It was a working day.
Thursday	I cycled to the park on my bike. It was a playing in the sun day.
Friday	I scooted to my friend's house on my scooter. It was a cooking day.
Saturday	I walked to the swimming pool. It was a swimming day.
Sunday	I stayed at home. It was a family day!

In the school holidays I did lots of exciting things. Read my diary.

2 Read the questions. Write answers in your notebook.

   a Did you do any of the things from the diary last week?

   b Which day sounds the most fun? Why?

3 Read these words.

   How many times can you find them in the diary?

went   to   walked   the   was   my

How are we doing?

Look in a reading book. See how many common words like *went*, *to*, *walked*, *the*, *was* and *my* you can find and read in 1 minute.

Ask someone to time you.

> 2.5 Retelling a diary

We are going to...

- **retell what happened in a week.**

Getting started

Play this game.

1 The class makes days of the week word cards.

2 In groups of seven, you each get a card with a day of the week on it.

3 Remember your day.

4 When you hear your day called out, clap loudly.

1 Retell the school holiday diary.

Use the pictures.

Speaking tip

Use this sentence frame to help you.

On _____ day we went to _____ on _____
_____ .

It was a _____ day.

2 Make a chart, like this.

   a Fill it in for each day of the week.

   b Write your answers as sentences if you can.

On Monday we went to the library on a bus. It was a reading day.

When?	Where?	How?	What?
Monday	to the library	on a bus	to read
Tuesday			

Writing tip

Look out for words in the past tense that end in –ed:

jump<u>ed</u>, play<u>ed</u>, stay<u>ed</u>, walk<u>ed</u>.

Look out for those that do not:

was, went, saw, read

3 Use the diary and the chart to help you say and write your answers.

   a When did the girl go to the swimming pool?

   b Where did she go on Wednesday?

   c How did she go to the park?

   d What did she do on her roller skates?

Writing tip

When, where, how and what often begin a question.

> 2.6 Writing a diary

We are going to...

- write a diary using and to join sentences.

Getting started

Talk about these diaries.

1   What do we use a diary for?
2   Which one would you choose?
3   Why?

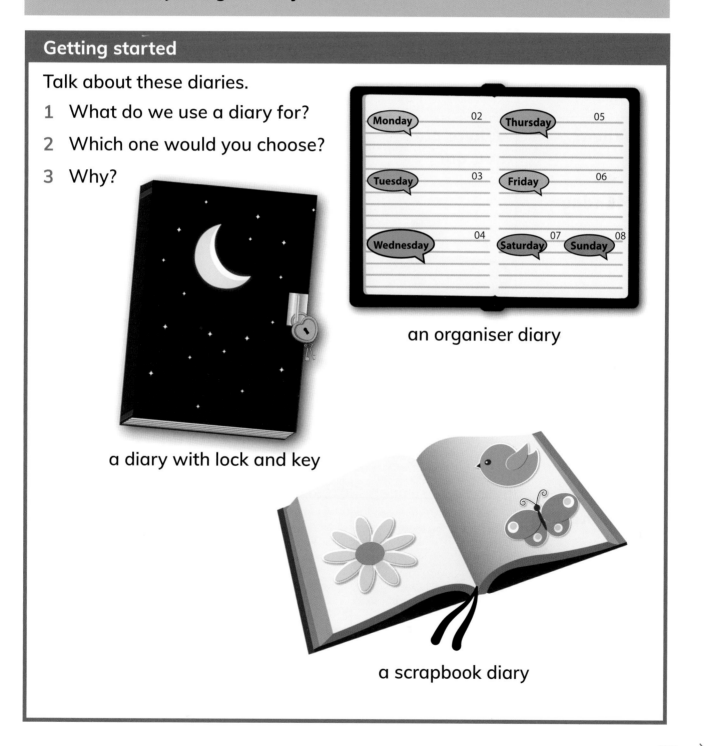

a diary with lock and key

an organiser diary

a scrapbook diary

Language focus

We can use **and** to join words and sentences together.

*On Tuesday I went to a café **and** I ate a sandwich. I went by car.*

1   Pretend this is your diary.

Talk about it with a partner.

Use the word 'and'.

When?	Where did you go?	What did you do?	How did you get there?
Monday			
Tuesday			
Wednesday			

When?	Where did you go?	What did you do?	How did you get there?
Thursday			
Friday			
Saturday			
Sunday			

On Monday I went to the park and I played football. I ran there.

2 Pick something from each column of the diary to make new sentences.

Mix up your ideas, like these.

> On Thursday I went to the café and played ping-pong. I went by plane.

> On Saturday I went to the cinema and I went swimming. I walked.

3 Fill in your own diary.

  a Draw pictures or write words to show what you did.

  b Say what you did.

  c Write about what you did on two days.

    On Monday I went to ____ ____ ____ and I ____ ____ ____ .

    I went there by / on ____ ____ ____ .

My diary			
When?	**Where did you go?**	**What did you do?**	**How did you get there?**
Monday			
Tuesday			

> Remember you can join your sentences with *and*.

> 2.7 A big day out

We are going to...

- **listen to, talk about and read a recount about a day out.**

Getting started

Look at the photos.

1   Which day out looks best?

2   Where do you like to go for a day out?

1   Listen to and read about Polly's day out in A *Trip* to a *Theme Park*.

Polly went with her friend Sal.

A Trip to a Theme Park

It was Polly's birthday. Sal and Polly went to a theme park, Cloud Nine.

They looked at the map to plan their day.

First, they went to see the dolphins and watched the show.

Next they saw the big roundabout.

Then they found the Slide and Glide.

A girl came down very fast and splashed.

At the end of the day they were tired so they sat in a café and rested.

They both had a drink with a straw and Polly got a Cloud Nine birthday bag.

It was a fantastic day out and they felt very happy.

Reading tip

Look for the full stops and remember to take a breath at each one.

2   Read this sentence out loud.

> They both had a drink with a straw and
> Polly got a Cloud Nine birthday bag.

a   Draw the birthday bag in your notebook.

b   Draw and write what you think was in the bag.

3   What else do you think happened at the theme park?

Use these pictures to help you.

I think it rained so they went inside to eat candyfloss.

I think Sal and Polly got lost.

61

> 2.8 Checking understanding

We are going to...

- **answer questions and retell a recount to check our understanding.**

Getting started

Look at each picture.

Which word describes each picture?

1   Read A *Trip* to a *Theme Park* again.

a   Match the questions with the answers.

1	Where did Sal and Polly go?	i	They felt very happy.
2	Why did they have a day out?	ii	At the end of the day.
3	What did they do first?	iii	First, they went to see the dolphins.
4	When did they sit in the café?	iv	They went to the Cloud Nine theme park.
5	How did they feel?	v	Because it was Polly's birthday.

b   Say each question and answer.

c   Write them in your notebook.

d   Now write your own question.

2   Sort the pictures into the correct order to retell A *Trip* to a *Theme Park*.

3   Make up an action for each thing Polly and Sal did at the theme park.

Use your actions to retell and act what the girls did.

› 2.9 Exploring words and writing a recount

We are going to...

- **explore and use words to help us write a recount.**

Key word

explore: to find out more about something.

Getting started

Look at these pictures and words.

1   Say the words.

2   Now say the words for more than one of each thing.

3   How did you change the words?

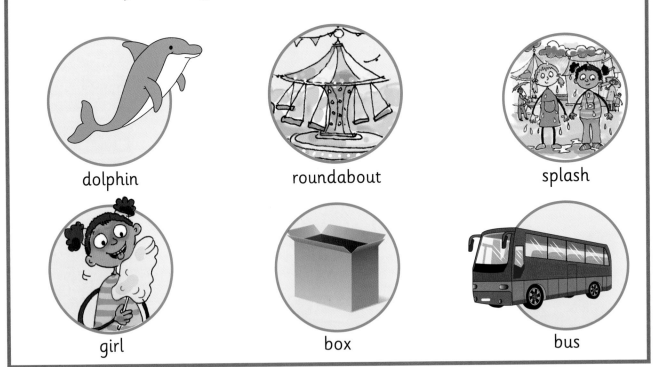

| dolphin | roundabout | splash |
| girl | box | bus |

Language focus

To change a **singular** noun to a **plural** add –s.

dolphin → dolphins

 →

singular → plural

If singular nouns end with –ch, –sh, –s, –x or –z, add –es.

box → box<u>es</u>

 →

singular → plural

 1 Listen to the sentences from A *Trip* to a *Theme Park*.

a Wave when you hear a word ending in –s.

b Clap when you hear a word ending in –es.

Listening tip

Close your eyes to help you listen carefully!

2 Read or listen to *A Trip to a Theme Park* again. Fill the gaps with these words. Use your notebook.

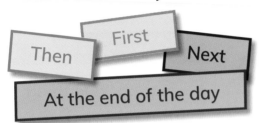

First

Then

Next

At the end of the day

These words help us to retell the story in the correct order. Try using them!

It was Polly's birthday. Sal and Polly went to a theme park, Cloud Nine. They looked at the map to plan their day.

_____, they went to see the dolphins and watched the show.

_____, they saw the big roundabout.

_____ they found the Slide and Glide.

A girl came down very fast and splashed.

___ ___ ___ ___ ___ ___ they were tired so they sat in a café and rested.

They both had a drink with a straw and Polly got a Cloud Nine birthday bag.

It was a fantastic day out and they felt very happy.

3 Make up a recount about a big day out.

a Use the ideas in the pictures in Session 2.7 or think of your own.

b Work with a partner to retell your big day out in the correct order.

c Now write your own recount.

❯ 2.10 Holiday news!

We are going to...

- **talk about sending holiday news.**

Getting started

Talk about these ways to tell people your news.

1   **Listen to and read about Jared. He is on holiday in Barbados with his mum and visiting his Grandma. He writes a postcard to his friends back in school to tell them his news.**

Dear Red Class,

How are you? I am having fun here.

I swim every day in a pool or the sea. Mum says I am turning into a fish! I say that I'd rather be a turtle.

Oh yes! I forgot to tell you that lots of the beaches here are turtle beaches. That means turtles lay their eggs on the beach and when the turtles hatch they have to scramble back into the sea to survive. Some babies don't make it to the sea and it's a bit sad. Perhaps I will be a fish after all!

Next week I am going to try body surfing!

See you all soon,

Jared.

p.s. Mum helped me to write this.

Red Class

Brighton Park School

Dolphin Street

Seatown ST2 4ET

2 Answer the questions about Jared's postcard.
Say or write your answers.

   a Who is Jared writing to?

   b Who is Jared visiting?

   c Did Jared remember to write the date on the postcard?

   d What did Jared nearly forget to tell?

   e How do you think Jared is feeling about his holiday in Barbados?

3 Point to these parts of the postcard.

Dear Red Class   See you all soon   P.S.

   a Which words are at the start of the postcard and which are at the end?

   b What does writing P.S. let you do?

   c Who would you write a postcard to?

Writing tip

In a postcard or letter you can write P.S. if you want to add something extra.

> 2.11 Planning and writing a postcard

We are going to...

- talk about, plan and write a postcard.

Getting started

Look at the features of letters and postcards.

1 Talk about the features.

> begins with *Dear* ...

> ends with **See you soon** if you are friends ...

> can end with **from** ...

> has space to write an address

> tells news

2 Did you see any other features in Jared's postcard to his friends?

1 Look at the pictures with a partner.

  a Talk about what else Jared is doing on holiday.

  b Add your own ideas.

2   Pretend you are Jared and you are writing a postcard to your class friends. Tell them about three special things. Write them in your notebook.

POSTCARD

PLACE
STAMP
HERE

First, I...

Then, I...

Next, I...

Finally, I...

DELIVER TO :

Brighton Park School,

Dolphin Street,

Seatown   ST2 4ET

FROM:

3 Write your postcard.
On one side write your message.
Use the three special things you
wrote in your notebook.
Write the address too.

You will need
paper or card like
a postcard.

Draw your stamp here.

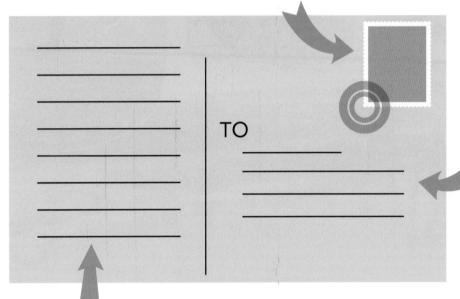

TO

Write your school
address here.

Write here.

On the other side of your postcard, draw a picture of one of the
three special things you have written about.

Draw your picture here.

> 2.12 Look back

We are going to...

- **check our writing and look back at our learning.**

Getting started

Talk about the letters in this writing.

1 What do you notice about the spacing of the letters and words?

2 Which looks best?

An owl and a crow in bows.
An owl and a crow in bows.

chicken and chips
chicken and chips

1 Check your writing.

  a Look at how you spaced your writing on your postcard.
Is your writing neatly spaced?

  b Read your postcard.

2 Look back at the recounts in this unit.

  a Talk about the recounts with a partner.
The titles are:

  My First Train Trip

  A Trip to a Theme Park

  Jared's postcard

  b Try to remember what each recount was about.

How are we doing?

Show your postcard to a partner. What do they think about it?

3. Say or write one thing you learned to help with these skills.

reading   writing   spelling   listening   speaking

How are we doing?

Which skill do you think you are best at? Why?

Look what I can do!

☐ I can explore different ways to tell people about things that have happened in the past.

☐ I can retell information from a recount.

☐ I can read recounts and answer questions.

☐ I can make an A–Z chart and say the days of the week.

☐ I can plan and write a postcard.

☐ I can check my writing and talk about my learning in the unit.

Check your progress

Answer the questions below to show what you have learned in this unit.

1 What is a recount?

2 Which word tells you when this happened?
   Yesterday I went on a train ride.

3 Say or sing the alphabet.

4 Finish the sequence: Monday, Tuesday ...

5 Join these two sentences together. *Jared swims every day.*
   Next week he is going to try body surfing!

6 How would you tell people about your holiday news?

Projects

Group project: Set up a class post office. Find or make all the things you need to go in it. For example, you might need some stamps and some envelopes or a sign to say your post office is open.

Pair project: Make an envelope by folding paper.
Write a letter to go inside.

Solo Project: For two weeks, write or draw something in a diary about what you have done each day.
Do you like writing a diary? You may decide to carry on!

3 ▶ Rhythm and rhyme

> 3.1 Finger rhymes

We are going to...

- **explore** rhymes and join in with a finger rhyme.

Key word

explore: to find out more about something

Getting started

Look at the picture.

Match the words in the box to the picture.

Do you know any of these rhymes?

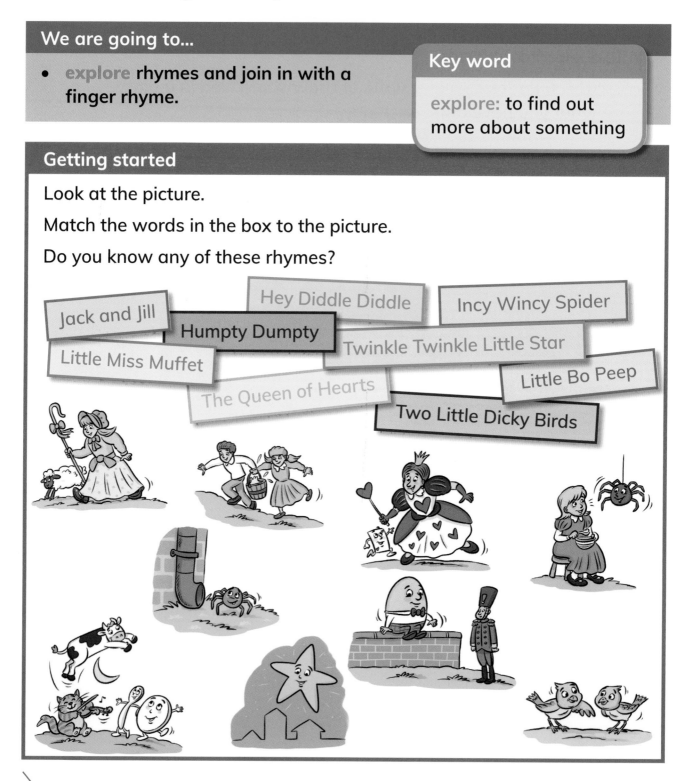

Jack and Jill

Hey Diddle Diddle

Incy Wincy Spider

Humpty Dumpty

Little Miss Muffet

Twinkle Twinkle Little Star

The Queen of Hearts

Little Bo Peep

Two Little Dicky Birds

1   Listen to and read *Fingers All*. It is an action rhyme.

Listen again. Use your fingers for the actions.

Fingers All

Theo Thumb, Theo Thumb,
Where are you?
Here I am. Here I am.
How do you do?

Pablo Pointer, Pablo Pointer,
Where are you?
Here I am. Here I am.
How do you do?

Tabby Tall, Tabby Tall,
Where are you?
Here I am. Here I am.
How do you do?

Rachel Ring, Rachel Ring,
Where are you?
Here I am. Here I am.
How do you do?

Baby Billy, Baby Billy,
Where are you?
Here I am. Here I am.
How do you do?

2 Talk about the rhyme.

a Which letters repeat in each finger name?

b Which words repeat?

c Which words rhyme?

d Which finger name do you like best?

e What would you name each finger?

3 Perform the rhyme.

a Try to say or sing it.

b Try to do the actions at the same time.

I can do *some* actions as I say the rhyme.

How are we doing?

Is it easy or difficult to say the words and do the actions at the same time?

› 3.2 Number rhymes

We are going to...

- **explore number rhymes and write rhyming words.**

Getting started

Count to ten!

Point to the numbers as you count.

Then read the number words.

1	**2**	**3**	**4**	**5**
one	two	three	four	five
6	**7**	**8**	**9**	**10**
six	seven	eight	nine	ten

1 Listen to and read these number rhymes.

   a Say them out loud.

   b Try the actions too!

One, Two, Buckle My Shoe

One, two, **buckle** my shoe.
Three, four, knock at the door.
Five, six, pick up sticks.
Seven, eight, lay them straight.
Nine, ten, a big fat hen.

Glossary

buckle: a pin used for joining the two ends of a strap.

Oliver Twist

Oliver – Oliver Twist
I bet you can't do this:
Number one – touch your tongue
Number two – touch your shoe
Number three – touch your knee
Number four – touch the floor
Number five – do a dive
Number six – build with bricks
Number seven – go to Devon.
Number eight – bang the gate
Number nine – walk in a line
Number ten – start again.

2 Say the rhymes with a partner.

Person one: Say the number words.

Person two: Finish the phrase.

Swap.

Person two: Say the number words.

Person one: Finish the phrase.

Try to do actions for the words you say!

> One, two …

> … buckle my shoe.

> Number one …

> … touch your tongue.

3 Find the rhyming pairs for the numbers one to ten.

Write them like this in your notebook.

Numbers	One, Two, Buckle My Shoe	Oliver Twist
1 one	-	tongue
2 two	shoe	shoe
3 three		

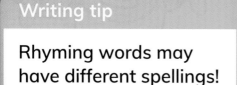

Writing tip

Rhyming words may have different spellings!

〉 3.3 Nonsense rhymes

We are going to...

- explore a nonsense rhyme and act it.

Getting started

Look at these pictures.

1 Point to the things that are nonsense.

2 Say why you think they are nonsense.

I think nonsense things are funny!

1 Listen to and read *Fire!*

Fire!

'Fire! Fire!' says Obadiah.
'Where? Where?' says Mrs Pear.
'Behind the rocks,' says Doctor Fox.
'Put it out!' shouts Mr Powt.
'I've no bucket,' says Miss MacTucket.
'Use my shoe,' says Betsy Lou.

2 Talk about the order of what happens in this rhyme.

Match the pictures with each line of Fire!.

a

d

b

e

c

f

3 Say and write the answer to each question.

Then think of some questions to ask a partner.

a What are the names of the people in the rhyme?

b Who is this? How do you know?

c What does Mrs Pear say?

d Does Miss MacTucket have a bucket?

e How many capital letters can you find in the rhyme?

4 Act the nonsense rhyme.

a Work in groups of seven.

- Six of you act each person in the rhyme.

- The seventh is a narrator.

b Talk about how you can make the rhyme funny.

Key word

narrator: the story teller.

I found 19 capital letters in the rhyme. Am I right?

We need a narrator to tell us the story of what is happening.

> 3.4 Exploring rhythm

We are going to...

- **use pictures to help us understand words we don't know.**

Getting started

Play a game of Me Then You.

- *I clap a rhythm.*
- *You clap the rhythm.*
- *I move in a rhythm.*
- *You copy me.*

What else has rhythm? Look at these photos for ideas.

1   Listen to *I Got the Rhythm* by Connie Schofield-Morrison.

   a   What do you notice about the rhythm of the poem?

   b   Listen again. Clap the rhythm when the poem pauses.

2   Now read the poem with rhythm.

   a   Look at the pictures.

   b   Work with a partner to add actions too.

I Got the Rhythm

I thought of a rhythm in my mind.
THINK THINK
I heard the rhythm with my ears.
BEAT BEAT
I looked at the rhythm with my eyes.
BLINK BLINK
I smelled the rhythm with my nose.
SNIFF SNIFF

I felt the rhythm with my knees.
KNOCK KNOCK
I walked the rhythm with my feet.
STOMP STOMP
I tapped the rhythm with my toes.
TIP TAP
I danced to the rhythm of a drum.
BEAT BOP

I clapped and snapped.

I tipped and tapped.

I popped and locked.

I hipped and hopped.

Connie Schofield-Morrison

3   Look at the chart.

   a   Match the pictures to the sentences
       to retell the story.

   b   Write each sentence in your notebook.

   c   Draw the matching pictures.

   d   Add the sound words in capital letters for each rhythm.

How are we doing?

How do the pictures help
you with your reading?

Picture	Sentence	Sound word for the rhythm
	1 I heard the rhythm with my ears.	BOOM BOOM
	2 I looked at the rhythm with my eyes.	BLINK BLINK
	3 I smelled the rhythm with my nose.	
	4 I felt the rhythm with my knees.	
	5 I walked the rhythm with my feet.	
	6 I tapped the rhythm with my toes.	
	7 I danced to the rhythm of a drum.	

Writing tip

Remember to use capital letters at the start of each sentence and for the sound words.

Z is a capital letter, but **z** is not!

› 3.5 Planning and writing a poem

We are going to...

- **plan and write a new poem using rhythm and rhyme.**

Getting started

Look at the colour charts.

Talk with a partner about different colours and the words we use for them.

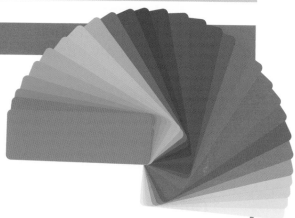

1 What is your favourite colour?

2 Why?

1   Listen to and read *Red is a Dragon* by Roseanne Thong.
    It is about colours.

   a   Listen for the rhythm.

   b   Listen for the words that rhyme.

Red is a Dragon

Red is a dragon
   Red is a drum
Red are the **firecrackers** –
   here they come!

Orange are the crabs
   that dance in the sand
And so is the seashell
   I hold in my hand

Yellow are raincoats
   and bright rubber boots
Yellow is a taxi
   that honks and toots

Green is a bracelet
   made of **jade**
Green is the purse
   my auntie made

Blue is a pool
   for making a wish
Dragonflies and
   shimmering fish

The world is a rainbow
   for us to explore
What colours are waiting
   outside your door?

Roseanne Thong

2 Write the answers to these questions.

   a How many verses does the poem have?

   b What do you notice about the pattern of this poem?

   c Clap the verses about red and blue. Is the rhythm the same or different?

   d What are the rhyming words in the poem?

   e What other colours do you think this rhyme should include?

3 Look at the colours in this chart.

   a Say what these colours make you think of.

   b Fill in a chart like this in your notebook.

   c Add your favourite colour to the chart.

Colours	What does the colour makes you think of?		
	1	2	3
purple	a night sky	a royal butterfly	plums
brown			
pink			
white			

4 Use your chart to write your own colour poem.

    a Look at this poem about purple using ideas from the chart.

    b Change the underlined words for your own ideas about your favourite colour.

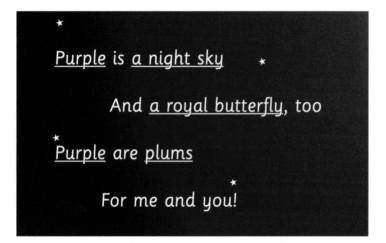

Purple is <u>a night sky</u>

And <u>a royal butterfly</u>, too

Purple are <u>plums</u>

For me and you!

Writing tip

Remember to use *is* or *are* in the right way!

We use *is* for one thing (singular).

We use *are* for two or more things (plurals).

› 3.6 Look back

We are going to...

- **check our writing and learning from this unit.**

Getting started

What do we look for when we 'check' our writing?

Say *yes* or *no*! Then say why.

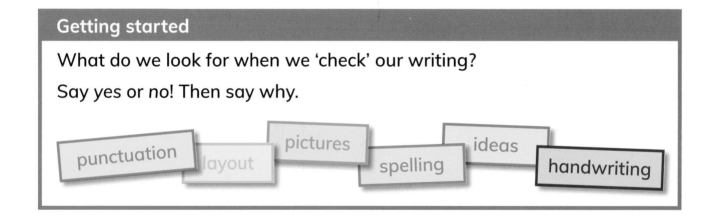

punctuation   layout   pictures   spelling   ideas   handwriting

1 Look at your ideas from your colour chart in Session 3.5 (Activity 3).

Did you remember to write a title for your new poem?

   a What do you think about your ideas? Talk about them.

   b Read your new poem about colour.

   c Share your poem to see what others think.

Listening tip

When others are speaking, sit still and look at them to show you are listening.

How are we doing?

Do pictures help you to remember things? Why?

2 Look back at all the rhymes in this unit.

   a Use the pictures to help you remember them.

   b Read or say each one.

3 Think about all the texts.

   a Which did you like best? Why?

   b Draw or write your answers.

How are we doing?

Check for mistakes or things you can improve.

Look what I can do!

- ☐ I can explore sounds, words and actions for rhymes.
- ☐ I can write rhyming words.
- ☐ I can act a nonsense rhyme.
- ☐ I can use pictures to help me understand words I don't know.
- ☐ I can plan and write a new poem using rhythm and rhyme.
- ☐ I can check my writing and talk about all the stories in the unit.

Check your progress

Answer the questions below to show what you have learned in this unit.

1 Say a word to rhyme with each of these words: *wish*   *day*   *pear*

2 Write a word that rhymes with *socks* but has a different spelling.

3 Read and clap the rhythm of this: *I looked at the rhythm with my eyes.*
BLINK BLINK

4 Spell the words for these numbers: 2   8

Projects

Group project: Make a poetry book. It should include all the types of rhyme in this unit. What sorts of rhyme will you share?

Pair project: Make a number or colour chart for the class.
Include some words with rhyme and/or rhythm.

Solo project: Make a small drum to practise rhythm.
What will you use to make it?

4 Joining-in stories

> 4.1 Off to tell the King

We are going to...

- **talk about, listen to and join in with a story.**

Getting started

Talk about these story characters.

1   What are their names and what stories are they in?

2   What other traditional tales do you know?

3   Who are the characters in those stories?

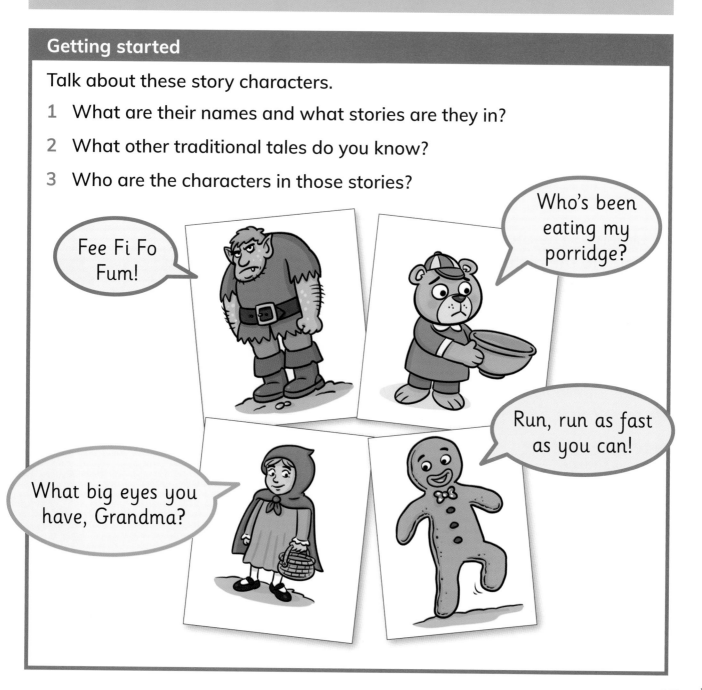

Fee Fi Fo Fum!

Who's been eating my porridge?

Run, run as fast as you can!

What big eyes you have, Grandma?

1 These characters are in *The Story of Chicken Licken*.
What do you notice about them? Say their names.

Chicken Licken

Hen Len

Cock Lock

Duck Luck

Turkey Lurkey

2 Listen to *The Story of Chicken Licken*.
Point to the pictures.

What birds do you see where you live?

 20 **The Story of Chicken Licken**

Chicken Licken has something important to tell the king.
He sets off. His friends join him one by one...

I will go to tell the King.

One day Chicken Licken was resting under a tree when ... PLOP!
The sun fell on him.
He was shocked.

On the way he met Hen Len.

On the way he met Cock Lock.

On the way he met Duck Luck.

97

On the way he met
Turkey Lurkey.

On the way he met Fox Lox.
And he gobbled them up!

3   Find the green words in the story.

   a   Read the green words aloud.

   b   Listen to the story again. Join in
       with the green words.

   c   Draw a picture of Chicken Licken in your
       notebook. Write the green words.

Reading tip

Remember to take a tiny
pause at the full stop.

> 4.2 Exploring language

We are going to...

- **answer questions and write sentences using *and*.**

Getting started

Try to remember the characters in *The Story of Chicken Licken*. Match the speech to the characters.

> I am a chicken. My name is Chicken Licken.

> I am a fox. My name is Fox Lox.

> I am a cockerel. My name is Cock Lock.

> I am a turkey. My name is Turkey Lurkey.

> I am a hen. My name is Hen Len.

> I am a duck. My name is Duck Luck.

1   Read each question. Say the answer then write it in your notebook.

What noises do these birds make?

a   Why was Chicken Licken shocked?

b   What really fell on Chicken Licken's head?

Language focus

We use **capital letters** for the names of characters.

We use a **full stop** at the end of sentences.

c   What did Fox Lox do?

2   Pick words from each box to write three sentences in your notebook.

Character	Verb	Who or where
Hen Len	tricked	with Chicken Licken.
Chicken Licken	went	under a tree.
Fox Lox	was resting	Chicken Licken and his friends.

3   Use the pictures to say who went with Chicken Licken.

a   Use the word *and* to add each character.

b   Write it as a very long sentence with lots of *and*s!

Language focus

We can use **and** to join phrases **or** sentences together.

Chicken Licken is going to tell the King.
Hen Len is going to tell the King.
Chicken Licken *and* Hen Len are going to tell the King.

> 4.3 Retelling and acting

We are going to...

- retell a story using pictures and masks.

Getting started

Look at the pictures.

Talk about the different ways we can retell a story.

I can make a mask to retell a story.

1   Use the pictures to retell *The Story of Chicken Licken.*
    Work with a partner.

Use these words and sentences to help you.

The sun fell on my head.
I am going to tell the King.

Will you come
with me/us?

Good
morning … !

2 Pretend you are Chicken Licken.

a Write one or two sentences in your notebook for each picture in Activity 1.

> **Writing tip**
>
> Remember to use phonics to help you spell. Sometimes, two or more letters make one sound
>
> D-u-ck L-u-ck.

The sun **fe**ll on my head and I'm going to te**ll** the Ki**ng**.

b Read your sentences. Talk about them with a partner.

3 Make a mask for each character in *The Story of Chicken Licken*.

a Work in groups to act the story. What will your character say? You could make puppets too!

> 4.4 Run, run as fast as you can

We are going to...

- **listen for repeated words and the order of events.**

Getting started

Read this poem. Talk about it.

Bread Man

Bread Man! Bread Man!	Roti for your Grandpa
Have you any bread?	Naans for your school
Yes, son! Yes, son!	And toast for that old man
The bread man said.	With his poor old mule!

- Do you buy bread or make it?

- What sort of bread do you eat?

1 Listen to *The Runaway Chapatti.*
In the story different characters join in to chase something.

   a As you listen, point to the people or animals who are chasing.

b Listen again for repeated words and join in when you can.

> **How are we doing?**
>
> What helps you to listen for repeated phrases or sentences?

2 Listen again. In your notebook, draw the characters in the order you hear them. Label them.

Little Anya

3 Draw The Chapatti Man in your notebook. Write what he says. Fill in the gaps. What is the same about the missing words?

Try joining some pairs of letters in the missing words.

Run, run as _____ as you can.
You can't _____ me – I'm
The Chapatti Man!

＞ 4.5 The pancake rolled on

We are going to...

- **talk about story characters and ideas.**

Getting started

Sing or say this traditional rhyme about pancakes.

Make up actions for each line.

Mix a Pancake

Mix a pancake,

Stir a pancake,

Put it in the pan.

Fry the pancake,

Flip the pancake–

Catch it if you can!

Christina Rossetti

1   What sort of pancakes do you eat where you live?

2   How do you make pancakes?

3   What do you eat them with?

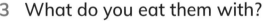

1 Listen to and read part 1 of *The Big Pancake* by Susan Gates and Alan Rogers.

How many times do you hear 'The pancake rolled …'?

The Big Pancake, Part 1

The cook made a big pancake.
But the pancake jumped out of the pan and rolled away.
'Come back,' said the cook.
The big pancake rolled on.

The pancake came to a house.
'Help me!' said a lady.
'Jump! I'll catch you!' said the pancake.
The pancake rolled on.

The cook and the lady ran after the pancake.
The pancake came to an enormous hole in the road.
'Help! My goats will fall into the big hole!' said the boy.
'I can help you!' said the pancake.
The pancake rolled on.

The cook, the lady and the boy ran after the pancake.
The pancake came to a river.
'Help! She can't swim!' said a girl.
'Climb onto me!' said the pancake.
The pancake rolled on.

Susan Gates and Alan Rogers

2 Read the story on your own or with a partner.

> **Reading tip**
>
> To help you read the words:
> * use your phonics
> * look at the pattern of repeated words and phrases
> * look at the pictures.

a Match the questions to the answers.
Write them in your notebook.

Question	Answer
1 What did the cook say about the pancake?	**A** He lay on top of the big hole in the road so the goats did not fall into it.
2 How did the pancake help the lady?	**B** He floated in the water for the girl to climb on.
3 How did the pancake help the boy?	**C** It's the biggest pancake I have ever seen.
4 How did the pancake help the girl?	**D** Because he thought they all wanted to eat him.
5 Why did the pancake keep rolling on?	**E** He let the lady land on him when she jumped out of the window.

b Why was the cook making a pancake?
Do you think the cook was going to eat it?

3 Read the Language focus box.

Choose *a*, *an* or *the* for each sentence.
Then write the sentences in your notebook.

a The cook made _____ big pancake.

b 'It's _____ biggest pancake I have ever seen!'

c The pancake jumped out of _____ pan and rolled away.

Language focus

We use:

- **the** before singular and plural nouns

- **a** or **an** before singular nouns when it does not matter which one we mean.

We do not use **a** or **an** before plural nouns or names.

> # 4.6 Story endings

We are going to...

- **read and write story endings.**

Getting started

Talk about story endings.

- How do these stories end?

- Which stories have a happy ending?

- Which stories have a sad ending?

1 Talk about these endings for *The Big Pancake*.
Which one do you think is best?

a

I think the pancake meets a fox and is gobbled up.

b

I think the pancake escapes!

c

I think the cook, the lady, the boy and the girls thank the pancake.

2 Read part 2 of *The Big Pancake*, the end of the story.

The Big Pancake, Part 2

The cook, the lady, the boy and the
little girls ran after the pancake.
The pancake came to a hill.
'I can't roll up a hill. I am too tired. You will
just have to eat me,' said the pancake.

'We don't want to eat you. We want
to say thank you,' they said.

Susan Gates and Alan Rogers

How are we doing?

What helps you to guess
the ending of a story?

Did you choose
the correct ending?
Was the ending a
surprise?

3 Draw and write new endings for the stories in Getting started.
Here are some ideas to help you.

> 4.7 Comparing stories

 26

We are going to...

- **talk about things that are the same and different in stories.**

Getting started

Sing *Roll Over!* You need to change the number for each verse.

- How is this story song the same as the stories you have read so far?

- How is it different?

What other stories or songs do you know that take away or add characters or things?

I can sing *Roll Over*. 'There were ___ in the bed, and the little one said Roll over, roll over!'

1   Talk about different ways to sort these stories.

Use these ideas to help you.

Sort by character   Sort by story events

Sort by beginning   Sort by ending

> **Key word**
>
> story events: things that happen in a story.

2   Copy the chart. Fill it in to show what is the same about the stories, and what is different. Work in a group.

Sorting stories	The Story of Chicken Licken	The Runaway Chapatti	The Big Pancake
By character	Animals – birds and a fox	Some people and a pretend thing	Some people and a pretend thing
By story beginning			
By story events			
By story ending			

3   In your group, choose two stories from your chart.

a   Say and write two things that are the same.

b   Say and write two things that are different.

> 4.8 Along skipped a boy with his whirly-twirly toy

We are going to...

- **explore words and language in part 1 of a story.**

Getting started

Talk about the names of these toys.

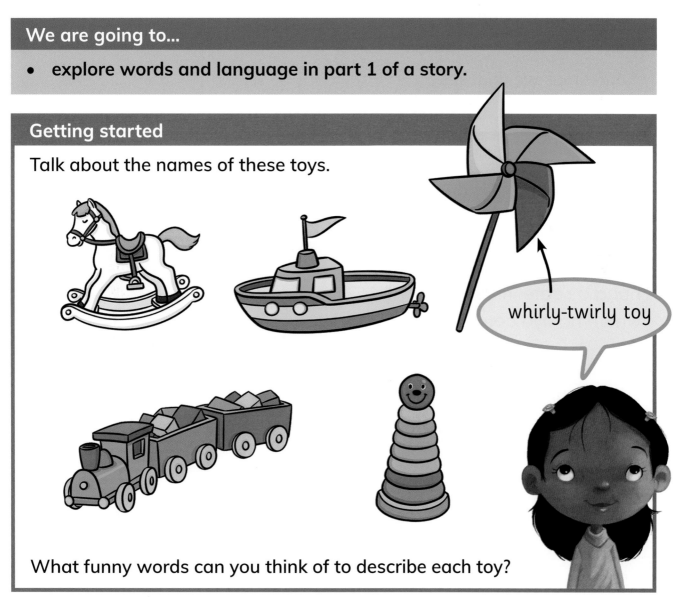

whirly-twirly toy

What funny words can you think of to describe each toy?

1   Listen to and read part 1 of *One Day in the Eucalyptus,*
    Eucalyptus Tree by Daniel Bernstrom.

    Point to each picture as you hear it.

    How many times do you hear 'whirly-twirly toy'?

Language focus

We can add –s to make things plural.

One toy.   **Lots of toys.**

Sometimes we add –es

box   **boxes**

Sometimes we add –ies

baby   **babies**

One Day in the Eucalyptus, Eucalyptus Tree, Part 1

One day in the leaves of
the eucalyptus tree
hung a scare in the air
where no eye could see,

when along skipped a boy
with a whirly-twirly toy,
to the shade of the eucalyptus,
eucalyptus tree.

Down, down
slid the snake
from the leaves
of the tree

and gobbled up the boy
with his whirly-twirly toy,
one day in the eucalyptus,
eucalyptus tree.

From inside the snake's dark and
deep tummy the boy then tempts
the snake to eat more.

Sneaky-slidey zipped the snake
And gobbled up the bird and her
ooey-gooey worm
one day in the eucalyptus,
eucalyptus tree.

Daniel Bernstrom

2 Listen again. Answer the questions.

a What was the boy doing?

b Where was the snake?

c What did the snake gobble first?

d What does snake hear?

running

skipping

in the tree   under the tree

the boy and the worm

the boy and the toy

a worm cheeping

a bird cheeping

3 Match the words to the pictures. Write and draw them in your notebook.

a ooey-gooey   b sneaky-slidey   c dark and deep

What do you think the snake does next?

> 4.9 Out dashed the cat

We are going to...

- **explore verbs and language in part 2 of a story.**

Getting started

What can you remember from part 1 of *One Day in the Eucalyptus, Eucalyptus Tree*?

1 What did the snake eat?

2 Name these animals.

3 Say the sounds you think they make.

Hiss, hiss

1 Listen to and read part 2 of *One Day in the Eucalyptus,*

Eucalyptus Tree. Point to each picture as you follow the story.

  a Listen for what else the boy tempted the snake to eat.

  b Did you guess correctly what the boy did to tempt the snake
  to eat more?

One Day in the Eucalyptus, Eucalyptus Tree, Part 2

Under-over slid the snake
and gobbled up the cat,
in his dozy-cozy nap,
one day in the eucalyptus,
eucalyptus tree.

Twist-twist bent the snake
from his place in the leaves
and gobbled up the ape and
her munchy bunch of grapes,
one day in the eucalyptus,
eucalyptus tree.

Up, up snaked the snake
And gobbled up the bear
With the qually-wally hair,
one day in the eucalyptus,
eucalyptus tree.

The snake went: Sniff, sniff. Gulp!
His tummy went: Gurgle-gurgle… blurble

Out ran the bear and out swung the ape,
Out dashed the cat and out flew the bird
with the ooey-gooey worm,

And out skipped the boy
with the whirly-twirly toy ...
one day in the eucalyptus,
eucalyptus tree.

Daniel Bernstrom

2   Read part 2 of the story again.

Sort the verbs.
Write them in two lists.

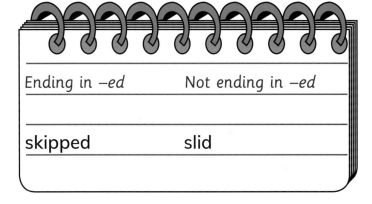

Ending in –ed	Not ending in –ed
skipped	slid

3   Work in pairs. One of you reads
the sentences. The other says
true or false.

a   The cat was teeny-tiny.

b   The ape was eating a munchy bunch of grapes.

c   The bear had qually-wally hair.

d   The bird was having a dozy-cozy nap.

Listening tip

Let others speak until the end of
their sentence. Then it's your turn.

How are we doing?

How well did you and your
partner take turns?

119

> 4.10 Joining in

We are going to...

- **join in with parts of the story and act it as a class.**

Getting started

Clap these words from the story.

eucalyptus   eu-cal-ypt-us

eucalyptus tree

in the eucalyptus tree

in the eucalyptus, eucalyptus tree

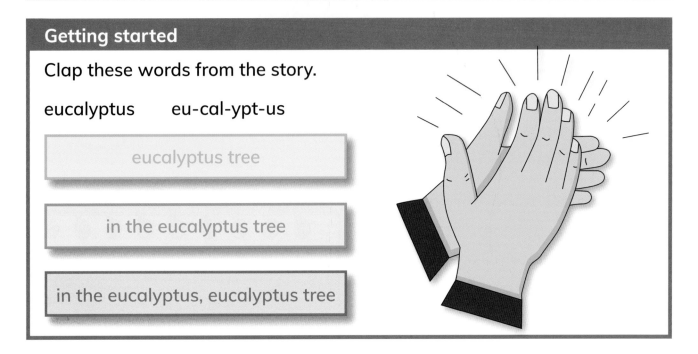

1   Listen to parts 1 and 2 of *One Day in the Eucalyptus, Eucalyptus Tree*. Join in.

Group 1: Join in with what the bird, cat and the ape say.

Group 2: Join in with the words that describe the snake's tummy.

Group 3: Say 'One day in the eucalyptus, eucalyptus tree'.

2 Act the story in a group. You will need these characters.

Make a big circle on the floor for the snake's tummy.

As the snake eats you, jump in the circle.

> 4.11 Planning and writing

We are going to...

- plan and write a joining-in story.

Getting started

Look at this eucalyptus tree.

It shows some of the animals that visit a eucalyptus tree in real life.

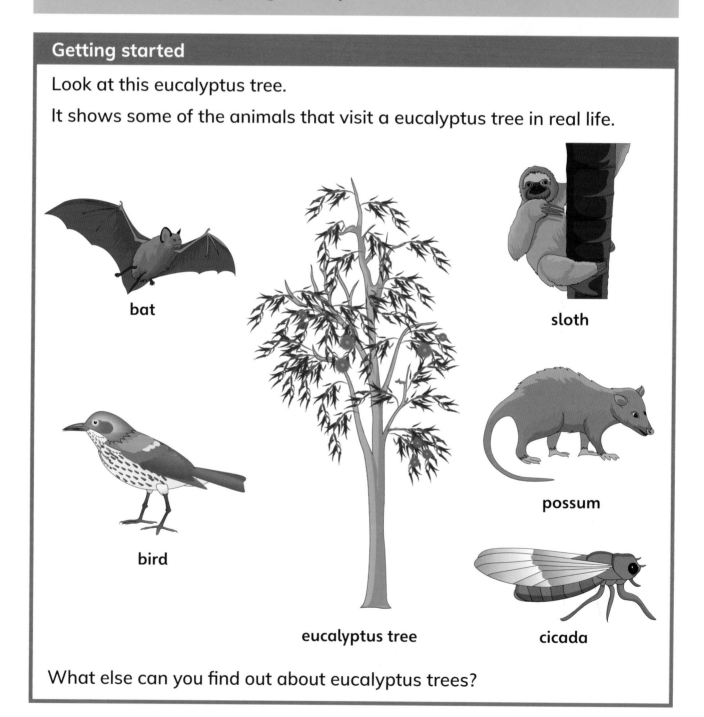

bat

sloth

possum

bird

eucalyptus tree

cicada

What else can you find out about eucalyptus trees?

1 You are going to write your own version of *In the Eucalyptus, Eucalyptus Tree*.

In pairs, choose what you want the snake to eat in your story. Use the ideas in Getting started to help you. Write your ideas in a planning chart like this.

In the story	boy and toy	bird and worm	cat	ape and grapes	bear
In our story					

2 Answer the questions to tell or write your story. Use **your** planning chart from Activity 1.

a Where was the snake?

b Who came skipping along?

c What did the snake do?

d What did the snake see and hear next? What did he do? Repeat this four more times. Choose different things for the snake to eat.

e What did the snake do because his tummy was so full?

f What came out of the snake's tummy?

3 Make your story into a poster. Use a large sheet of paper to write the words. Add pictures and sound words in speech bubbles.

A koala bear might make a sound like grunt-grunt and it might be chomp-chomping!

> 4.12 Look back

We are going to...

- **check our writing and look back at our learning.**

Getting started

Ask and answer questions about your story posters.

Use these question to help you.

1   Why did you ...?

2   What made you think of ...?

3   How did you ...?

1   Check your writing.

   a   Find one spelling mistake.

   b   Find one word you can write better. How?

   c   Find a word that has two letters that make one sound.

   d   Join the two letters that make one sound.

   bees   bees

   e   What would you change about your poster? Why?

How are we doing?

Did you remember to check capital letters and full stops?

2 Talk about all the stories and poems in this unit.

   a Which story and rhyme did you like best? Why?

   b Which story and rhyme did you like least? Why?

   c Which character did you like best? Why?

   d Which character did you like least? Why?

   e Which story would you read again?

> I liked the *Runaway Chapatti* because it was just like *The Gingerbread Man* story.

3 Say or write one thing you learned to help with these skills.

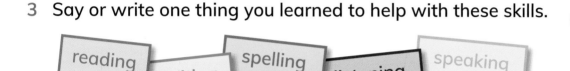

reading   writing   spelling   listening   speaking

> Joining in with stories helps me with my reading.

Look what I can do!

- ☐ I can explore different stories and compare them.
- ☐ I can retell stories in different ways.
- ☐ I can talk about story characters, settings and events.
- ☐ I can talk about and write story endings.
- ☐ I can plan and write a story like one I know.
- ☐ I can check my writing and talk about my learning in the unit.

Check your progress

Answer the questions below to show what you have learned in this unit.

1   What sort of stories have we read in this unit?

2   What did *The Runaway Chapatti* say each time he met someone?

3   Say one way that all the stories were similar.

4   Which story ending did you like the best?

5   Write these words as plurals: boy   fox

6   Join two short sentences to make one new sentence.

   The Chapatti Man jumped up.   The Chapatti Man ran away.

Projects

Group project: Make some pancakes, chapatti or gingerbread men. They can be real or pretend!

Pair project: Design and make a storytelling card game. Draw your story pictures on pieces of card. Put them in order as you tell the story.

Solo Project: Design and make a bookmark about the stories in this unit.

5 Do it like this!

> 5.1 Information all around us

We are going to...

- talk about, listen to and read information around us.

Getting started

Instructions can:

1 guide us, or

2 order us to do something.

Talk about the different instructions in these pictures.

Continued

Now talk about these instructions for how to make something.

Recipe:

How to make chocolate-chip muffins

What to do:

1   Put in the flour.
2   Put in the baking powder. Mix.
3   Put in the sugar.
4   Put in the choc chips. Mix.
5   Put in the eggs. Mix.
6   Put in the milk. Mix.
7   Bake the muffins in the oven.

What other instructions can I think of?

1   Talk about this map.

   a   Read the labels and signs. What do they tell you?

   b   What else could you label?

You might need to add a sign more than once.

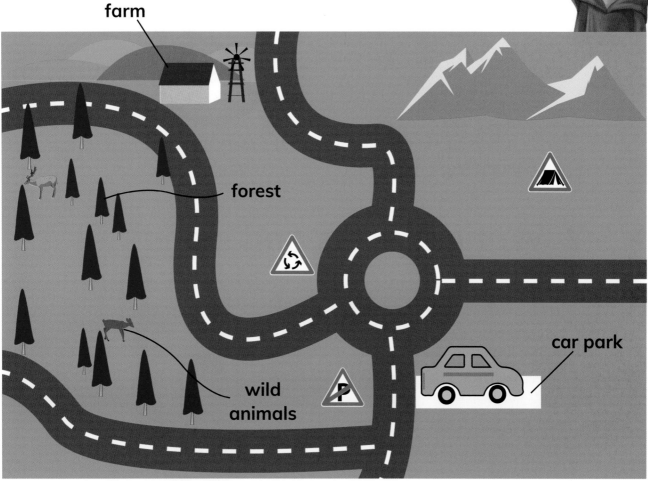

2   a   Say what you think these signs mean.

   b   Find the signs on the map or choose where to put them on the map.

3 Draw other signs you could add to the map.

a Think about the shape.

b Say what information your signs are giving or what they are telling people to do.

It tells us that ducks might cross the road.

It orders us not to take pictures.

〉 5.2 Writing labels and signs

We are going to...

- **make signs and write signs using capital letters.**

Getting started

What do these signs tell you?

1 Work with a partner.

2 Choose a sign and act it.

3 Ask your partner to guess what it means.

4 Swap.

I can make signs using my body and face.

1 Talk about these signs.

Answer the questions with a partner.

a What do you notice about the letters in these signs?

b Where might you see each sign?

c What does each sign tell you?

How are we doing?

How can we make sure people notice something?

Sometimes we use capital letters. What else can we do?

Writing tip

Here are all the capital letters in the English alphabet.

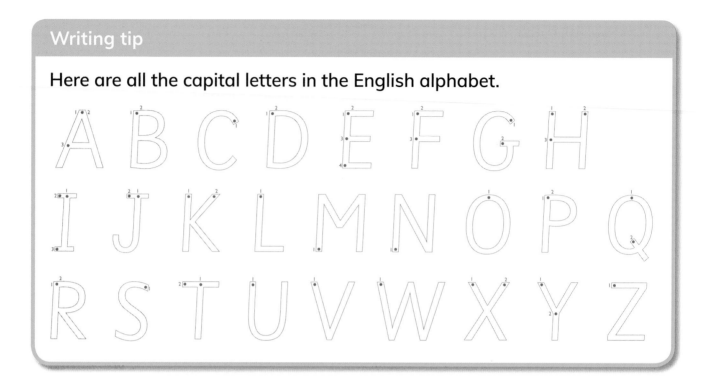

2   Design and write a sign using capital letters. Use a chart like this.

Think about these things.

Design	What it is for
Shape: round square triangle Other	What does your sign mean?
Colour: background and letters	Who is it for?
Letters: capital letters or lower case	Where will you put it?
Pictures or symbols	

How are we doing?

Are you pleased with your sign?

What do you like?

What would you change next time?

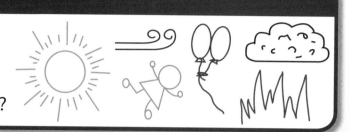

3   Describe your sign.

Speaking tip

Stand tall and smile.

Speak with a loud, clear voice.

My sign is for the classroom. It shows where the drawing table is. It is square. It uses coloured pictures and capital letters. I will hang it over the table.

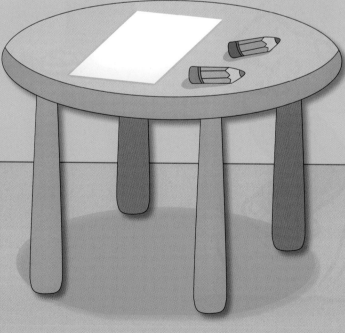

> 5.3 How to mix colours

We are going to...

- talk about, listen to and read about how to mix colours.

Getting started

Play a game.

Stand up if you are wearing red!

Hop if you are wearing blue!

Jump if you are wearing yellow!

What other colour games do you know?

1 Say the names of the colours.

   a Match the paint to the paint brush.

   b Draw the colours in your notebook and label them.

2 Look for colours around you.

   a Write a list of five colours.

   b Tick each colour when you find something that matches.

   c Draw what you find and label it.

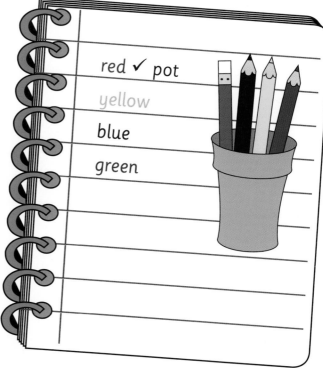

red ✓ pot
yellow
blue
green

3   Read the instructions for making colours.

Listen for the three colours that are mixed.

1 How to make orange.

Mix red and yellow to make orange.

2 How to make green.

Mix yellow and blue to make green.

3 How to make purple.

Mix blue and red to make purple.

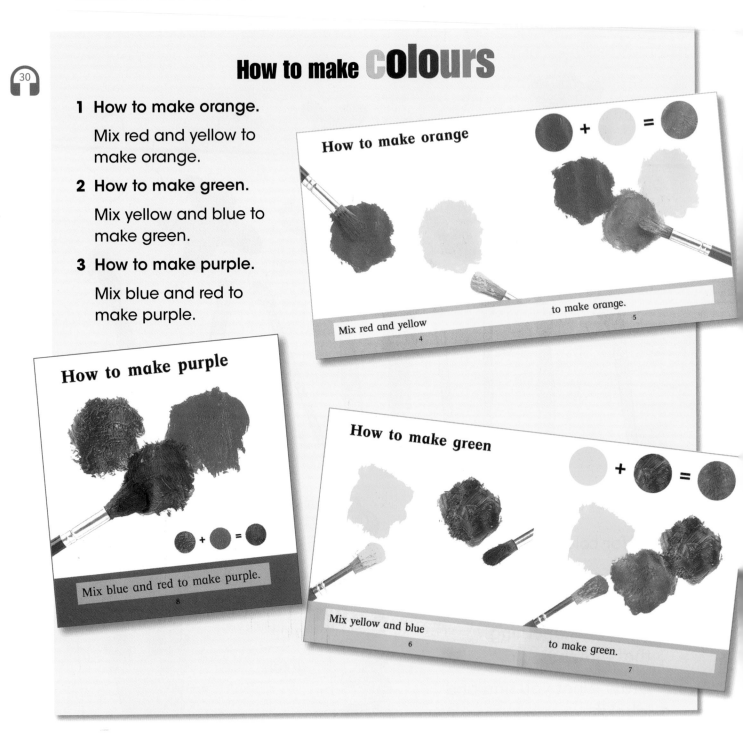

How to make **colours**

How to make orange

Mix red and yellow   to make orange.
4   5

How to make purple

Mix blue and red to make purple.
8

How to make green

Mix yellow and blue   to make green.
6   7

> 5.4 Checking understanding

We are going to...

- **answer questions to check we understand.**

Getting started

Play a game.

Mix up some colour cards.

Which colours can you make?

1   Answer the questions.
    Write the answers in your notebook.

    a What is this?

    b What do you need it for?

c Do you need blue paint to
   make orange?

d Do you need red to make purple?

e How do you make green?

f What do you think happens if you add
   white to red?

g What question would you like to ask
   about colours?

2 Write the sentences and fill in the gaps.

How to make colours

You need paint brushes _____ paint.

You _____ paper too!

1 How to _____ orange.

Mix red and yellow _____ make orange.

2 How _____ make green.

_____ yellow and blue to make green.

3 How to _____ purple.

Mix blue _____ red to make purple.

3 Copy the chart.

Sort the words.

Write the words into sets.

Choose the same underlined letters and the same sound.

gr<u>ee</u>n	yell<u>ow</u>	p<u>ur</u>ple	bl<u>ue</u>
			true

Look out!
You may not need to
use all the words

How are we doing?

What is different about
the ow in the words yell<u>ow</u>
and <u>how</u>?

> 5.5 Making a poster

We are going to...

- explore the features of an instructional text and make a poster.

Getting started

Talk about the features of an instructional text.

Point to or talk about the features.

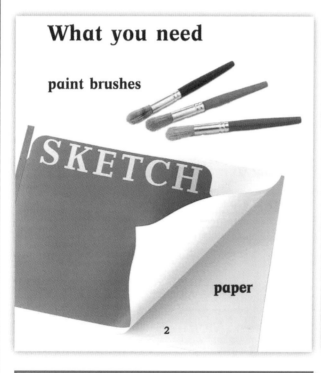

| Labels to name things you need. | Verbs that tell you what to do. |

| Photos of what you need. | Photos or pictures to tell you what to do. |

Ummm! What could I add to make sure you mix the colours in order?

1 Listen and point to these pictures in the correct order.

How are we doing?

What do you do to help you listen carefully?

Listening tip

Use numbers for instructions. Numbers make instructions easy to follow when you listen.

2 Look at these instructional posters.

Talk about how you would finish them.

How to get ready for painting

What you need:

What you do:

How to tidy up

What you need:

What you do:

3 Make a poster for your classroom.

a Work with a partner.

b Think about the features you will use to make the instructions clear.

c Make it fun so people want to read it!

Speaking tip

Listen to others in your group when you are sharing ideas.

> 5.6 Listening – from fiction to non-fiction

We are going to...

- talk about fiction and non-fiction texts.

Getting started

Say if you think these are story, poem or information books.

1 How do you know?

2 Which book would you choose to read?

3 Why?

1 Listen to part 1 of a story about a boy who likes folding things!

    a Point to the pictures as you listen.

    b Write any interesting words you hear or that
        you are not sure about.

Did you hear the word *origami*? It means folding paper into shapes.

2 Answer the questions about the story.

   a What did Joey love?

   b What did Sarah's mother do with paper?

   c What did Joey do? Why?

   d Where did he practise?

   e What did he make?

   f How do the pictures in Activity 1 tell you how Joey is feeling?

   g Write your own question about the text. Use your notebook.

3 Talk about *More-igami*.

   a Is it a fiction or non-fiction book?

   b How do you know?

   c Make a collection of books that have more than a story or information in them.

〉 5.7 How to make a ladybird

We are going to...

- **read instructions to make something.**

Getting started

Name these shapes.

Count them and write the answer in your notebook.

Point to a shape corner.

Point to a shape side.

1 Listen to and read part 2 of *More-igami* by Dori Kleber.

It tells you how to fold your own ladybird.

More-igami, Part 2

Fold your own origami ladybird.

Are you ready to make origami? Try this ladybird.
Keep practising until it's just right.

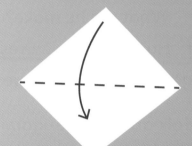

1 Start with a square of paper. Fold it in half
to make a triangle.

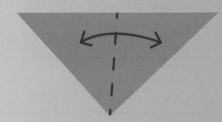

2 Fold the triangle in half. Press down hard
to make a crease, then open it back up.

3 Now fold the top corners down
to make the wings.

4 Add some spots to the wings.

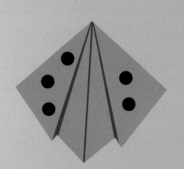

Dori Kleber

2   Write a list of verbs in the instructions.

3   Make your own origami
    ladybird.

    a Work with a partner or group.

    b You will need a square of paper 15 cm x 15 cm.
       That's about the width of this book.

    c Follow the instructions from Activity 1.

Can you fold the
paper to make a head
for the ladybird?

I remember... verbs
are words that tell you
what to do!

Reading tip

Use the numbers (1–4) to help you do things in the correct order.

Use the verbs and pictures to help you understand what to do.

> 5.8 Writing and sorting instructions

We are going to...

- **match and write instructions.**

Getting started

Talk about these origami models.

1   Which would you like to make?

2   Why?

1   Talk about these picture instructions.

   a   What are they showing you how to make?

   b   What is each picture telling you to do?

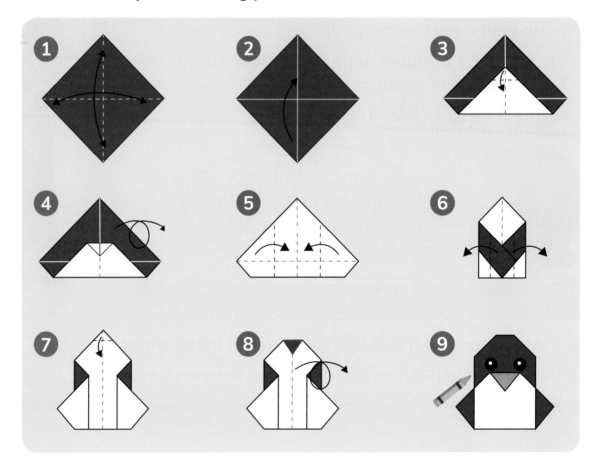

2   Match the instructions to the correct pictures in Activity 1.

   a   Fold the square in half from top to bottom and from side to side.

   b   Fold the sides in.

   c   Colour the beak. Enjoy your penguin!

3   Now write the first and the last instruction in your notebook
   and draw the penguin.

> 5.9 Instructions for cooking

We are going to...

- **explore the language of cooking instructions.**

Getting started

Look at the pictures.

All these things are needed to make something.

Can you guess what?

Sort the things into two sets:

1 **ingredients:** food you need

2 **equipment:** kitchen things you need

1¾ cups of sugar

2 eggs

apron

measuring jug

1 cup of milk

3 teaspoons (tsp.) of baking powder

2½ cups of flour

spoon

½ cup of oil

bowl

6 handfuls of choc-chips

1 Listen to the cooking instructions.

Then read the text aloud with a partner.

How to make muffins

1 Put in the eggs.

2 Put in the oil.

3 Put in the milk. Mix.

4 Put in the sugar. Whisk.

5 Put in the flour and baking powder. Mix.

6 Put in the choc-chips.

7 Bake the muffins in the oven.

Reading tip

If you can't read a word, try asking a partner for help.

2 Add the word *and* to steps 3, 4 and 5.

Do this to make each step into one sentence.

Are the instructions clearer as two sentences or one? Why?

We say *recipes* like this: *ressipeez*.

3 Look at the full stops in the **recipe**.

Talk about where you can see the full stops.

Glossary

recipes: instructions for how to cook things.

Language focus

We use full stops:

- at the end of sentences
- sometimes after numbers in a list
- for words we shorten: teaspoon → tsp.
- sometimes for people's titles: Mrs Takimoto.

> 5.10 Checking sequence

We are going to...

- **talk about correct order and check our understanding.**

Getting started

Play the game Jump in the Bowl!

Pretend you are the ingredients for making muffins.

Don't jump in the bowl until it is your turn!

1 Why does the order matter in a recipe?

2 How do we know what to do in which order?

1 Answer the questions about the muffin recipe in Session 5.9.

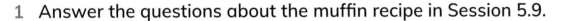

a What is the word for all the food we need for a recipe?

b Look at the photo. What is it? What is it for?

c Do you put in the eggs before the sugar?

d What is the first instruction in the recipe?

e What is the last instruction in the recipe?

f What do you think you need to do before you start to cook?

Make up another question to ask a partner.
Then swap and answer your partner's question.

2 Read the recipe again.

a Find the four verbs in the recipe that tell you what to do.

b Think of different verbs to use each time.

3 Write the instructions with your new verbs.

Writing tip

Try to use more interesting verbs like *add, beat, cook and stir.*

> 5.11 Planning and writing a recipe

We are going to...

- talk about, plan and write a recipe.

Getting started

Look at this table.

Talk about:

1 the features of a recipe

2 anything else you noticed about the recipe.

Does it...?	Yes or no?
begin with **Dear**...?	
have a clear heading?	
give instructions in the past tense?	
use numbers to give instructions in the correct order?	
list things you need?	
have pictures or photos?	

1 Write a chart to show the features of a recipe.

   Use the one in Getting started to help you plan.

How are we doing?

Keep your chart safe so you can use it to check your own recipe writing.

2 Pretend you are making muffins.

   a Change the choc-chips to make a different sort of muffin.

   b Write the new ingredient in your notebook.

I would add cherries.

I would add honey and apple.

3 Plan your recipe using these headings.

   Talk about your plan.

> **How to make** _____
>
> **Ingredients**
>
> **Equipment**
>
> **What to do:**

4 Write your recipe.

Writing tip

If you don't know how to write a word:

- try to work it out using phonics
- look around your classroom to see if there is something to help you
- ask for some help.

› 5.12 Look back

We are going to...

- **check our writing and talk about all the different instructions in the unit.**

Getting started

Talk about these different sets of instructions.

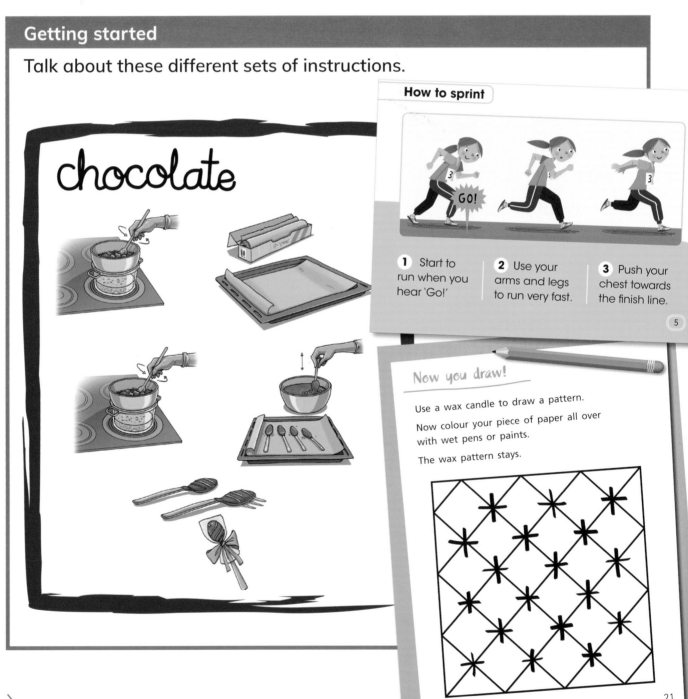

chocolate

How to sprint

1 Start to run when you hear 'Go!'

2 Use your arms and legs to run very fast.

3 Push your chest towards the finish line.

5

Now you draw!

Use a wax candle to draw a pattern.

Now colour your piece of paper all over with wet pens or paints.

The wax pattern stays.

21

1 Check your writing using the features chart you made (Session 5.11).

   a Did you use all the features?

   b Why?

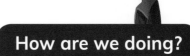

I added pictures and photos to my recipe? Did you remember to do this, too?

2 Look back at all the instructional texts in this unit.

   a Talk about them with a partner. Use the photos to help you.

   b Try to remember what each one told you to do and how.

How are we doing?

Share your recipe and see what others think.

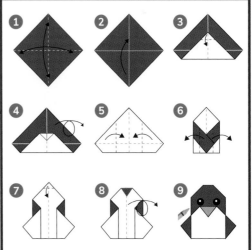

3 Say or write one thing you learned to help with these skills.

reading   writing   spelling   listening   speaking

Look what I can do!

☐   I can explore instructions.

☐   I can talk about different kinds of books.

☐   I can answer questions about instructions.

☐   I can read and write instructions.

☐   I can plan, write and check my writing.

☐   I can talk about my learning in the unit.

Check your progress

Answer the questions below to show what you have learned in this unit.

1   What can you use to make instructions clear?

2   Show a sign to tell someone that you want them to stop.

3   Which verbs tell you **what** to do? *Turn on the tap and wash off the soap.*

4   Join these instructions together to make one sentence:

   Stand it up. Pull out the side corners. Refold them so they stick out.

5   What are some of the ingredients for making muffins?

6   How would you explain what these words mean?
    label   origami   equipment   recipe

Project

Group project: Set up a class cooking club. Collect recipes and ask if you can make some of them. You don't always need an oven!

Pair project: Design and make a play mat.
Make buildings and signs.

Solo project: Find and follow instructions to make another origami model. Say if you found the instructions clear and what you would add to make them clearer.

6 ▸ Rhyme time

> 6.1 Our senses

We are going to...

- explore sounds and words in rhyming poems about our senses.

Getting started

Look at the pictures. What are the children doing?

1   Match the body parts to the correct word.
    Draw and write them in your notebook.

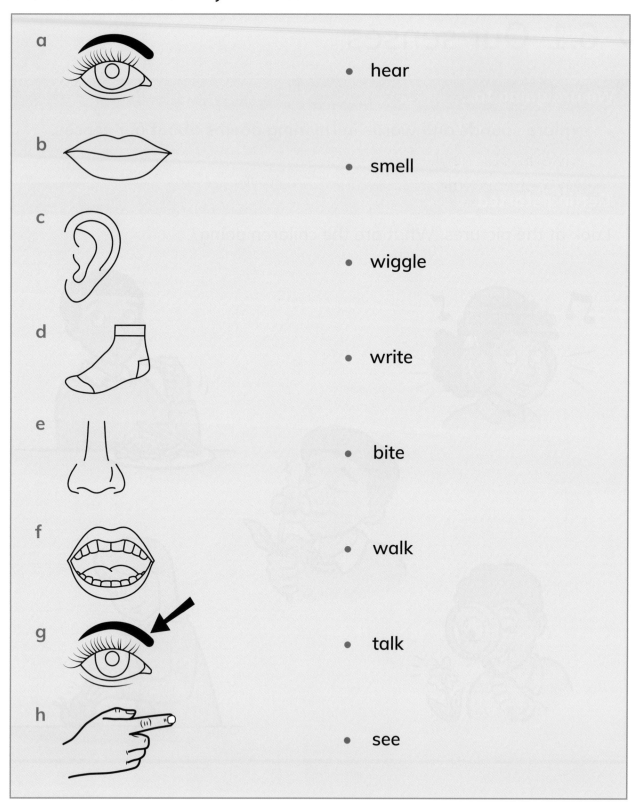

a

b

c

d

e

f

g

h

- hear

- smell

- wiggle

- write

- bite

- walk

- talk

- see

2 Listen to this rhyme. Point to each part of your body.

Read the rhyme and point again.

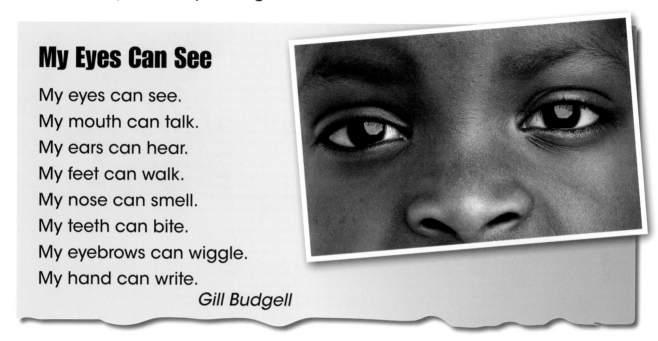

My Eyes Can See

My eyes can see.
My mouth can talk.
My ears can hear.
My feet can walk.
My nose can smell.
My teeth can bite.
My eyebrows can wiggle.
My hand can write.

Gill Budgell

3 Say what else your body parts can do.
Use verbs that are different from the poem.

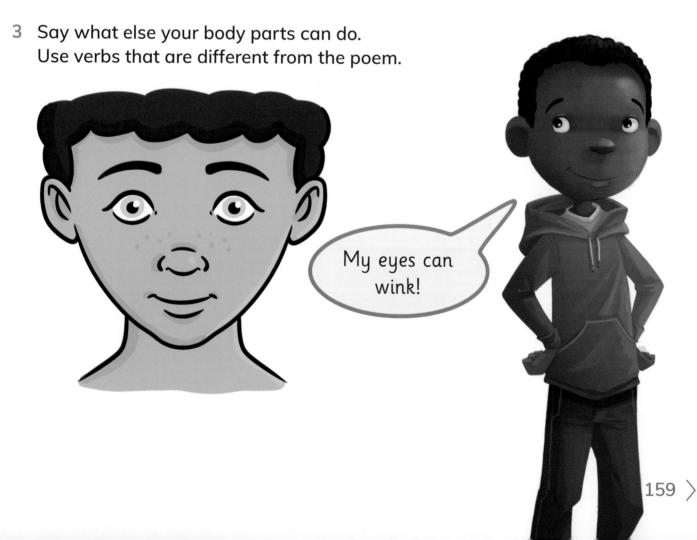

My eyes can wink!

4   Play a game of *I spy* ...

 36

I spy with my little eye ...

... something that is red.

I spy with my little eye ...

... something beginning with the *letter M.*

 37

I hear with my little ear ...

... something beginning with the letter sound *mmmm.*

I hear with my little ear ...

... something that rhymes with the word *door.*

How are we doing?

Which senses do you use to read?

> 6.2 Touch

We are going to...

- explore words and rhyming poems about touch.

Getting started

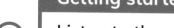

Listen to the action poem *Hands Up*. It is about using our hands to touch.

1 How many times do you hear the word touch?

2 Listen again and join in with the actions.

1   Listen to and read *Sand in …* by John Foster.
    It is a poem about touching and feeling sand.

    Make up actions for each line of the poem.

Sand in…

Sand in your fingernails
Sand between your toes
Sand in your earholes
Sand up your nose!

Sand in your sandwiches
Sand in your bananas
Sand in your bed at night
Sand in your pyjamas!

Sand in your sandals
Sand in your hair
Sand in your jumper
Sand everywhere!

John Foster

The words *toes* and *nose* rhyme!

2   Write the answers to the questions.
    Use your notebook.

    a   What is the poem about?

    b   How many times is the word *sand* used in the rhyme?

    c   Which are the rhyming words in each verse?
        Copy this chart and fill it in.

toes	bananas	hair

3 Listen to and read *Sand* by Shirley Hughes.

Does this poem rhyme?

Sand

I like sand.
The run-between-your-fingers kind,
The build-it-into-castles kind.
Mountains of sand meeting in the sky,
Flat sand, going on for ever,
I *do* like sand.

Shirley Hughes

Reading tip

This little line - is called a **hyphen**. You can use it to join words together like this: *build-it-into-castles*.

4 Write a sentence about the kind of sand you like. Use your notebook.

I like the _____-_____-_____-_____ kind.

I'm using this to help me think: 'The run-between-your-fingers kind'.

I like the stick-to-your-feet kind.

> 6.3 Feeling sad

We are going to...

- **explore words and rhyming poems about feeling sad.**

Getting started

Look at these pictures. Talk about how you think the girl is feeling.

Use some of the words to help you.

Sometimes it is tricky to work out how people are feeling.

1   Read *Sad Today* and *Sick*.
    Talk about how the children in these poems are feeling.

Sad Today

I'm feeling very sad today,

I've no idea what to say.

I wish you'd all go away

And leave me to be sad today.

My mum says that it's okay

To sometimes have a sad day

Because if we never have a sad day

How will we spot a glad day?

Gill Budgell

Sick

Hot, cross, aching head,

Prickly, tickly, itchy bed.

Piles of books and toys and puzzles,

Heavy on my feet,

Pillows thrown all anyhow,

Wrinkles in the sheet.

Sick of medicine, lemonade,

Soup spooned from a cup.

When will I be better?

When can I get up?

Shirley Hughes

165 〉

2 Write the rhyming words from each poem in sets like this.
Use your notebook.

Sad Today

> rhymes with day
>
> today / say

> rhymes with sad

Sick

> rhymes with bed
>
> head

> rhymes with up

> rhymes with feet

3 Read *Sick* again. Say and write the answers
to these questions.

a Which words tell you about the girl's head?

b Which words tell you about the girl's bed?

c What are there *piles* of?

d How does she feel about *medicine*,
lemonade and *soup*?

e What does she want to do?

> I pull the
> sheets over my head
> when I feel sick.

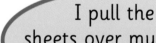

4 Work as a class to make an A–Z of feelings.

• Make 26 paper flags.

• Write a letter of the alphabet on each flag.

• Then write a feeling for that letter.

angry a | brave b | cross c | d | e | f | g | h

> 6.4 Feeling happy

We are going to...

- **explore words and rhyming poems about feeling happy.**

Getting started

Look at this picture and talk about the questions.

1 How are the children feeling? Why?

2 Where are they?

3 What are they doing?

Write a question about the picture to ask a partner.

Take turns to ask a partner these questions.

- How old are you?

- When is your birthday?

- Will you have a party?

Don't forget to begin your question with a capital letter.

1   Listen to and read *Laughing Time* by William Jay Smith.

Is it about feeling sad or happy? How do you know?

Laughing Time

It was laughing time, and the tall Giraffe
Lifted his head, and began to laugh:
Ha! Ha!   Ha! Ha!

And the Chimpanzee on the gingko tree
Swung merrily down with a Tee Hee Hee:
Hee! Hee!   Hee! Hee!

'It's certainly not against the law!'
Croaked Justice Crow with a loud guffaw:
Haw! Haw!   Haw! Haw!

The dancing Bear who could never say 'No'
Waltzed up and down on the tip of his toe:
Ho! Ho!   Ho! Ho!

The Donkey daintily took his paw,
And around they went: Hee-Haw! Hee-Haw!
Hee-Haw!   Hee-Haw!

The Moon had to smile as it started to climb;
All over the world it was laughing time!
Ho! Ho! Ho! Ho!   Hee-Haw! Hee-Haw!
Hee! Hee! Hee! Hee!   Ha! Ha! Ha! Ha!

William Jay Smith

How are we doing?

What did you do to listen to the poem well?

Language focus

Verbs can end with –s, –ing and –ed.

Verb	–s	–ing	–ed
laugh	She laughs	She is laughing She was laughing	She laughed
dance	He dances	He is dancing He was dancing	He danced

Not danceing.

Not danceed.

2 Read *Laughing Time* again. Then read the Language focus box. Write the verb endings in your notebook.

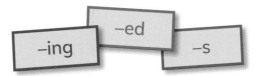

a The Chimpanzee is chatter_____ up high on the gingko tree.

b He is swing_____ merrily down with a 'Tee Hee Hee'.

c 'It's certainly not against the law!' croak_____ Justice Crow with a loud guffaw.

d The Bear and the Donkey were hold_____ hands and dance_____ .

e The Moon smile_____ as it started to climb.

3 List the pictures in the correct order with a partner. Read the poem to check.

a

b

c

d

e

f

4 Work in a group to read *Laughing Time* out loud.

- You will need five people in each group.
- Each person reads one verse.
- Read the last verse together.
- You can laugh in different ways!

Speaking tip

Before you speak:
- stand up tall
- smile
- take a deep breath
- say each word slowly and clearly
- speak with a strong, loud voice.

› 6.5 Planning and writing a rhyme

We are going to...

- plan and write a new rhyme about good and bad days.

Getting started

Say or sing the days of the week.

1 What makes a good day for you?

2 What makes a bad day?

3 How can we show our feelings without using words?

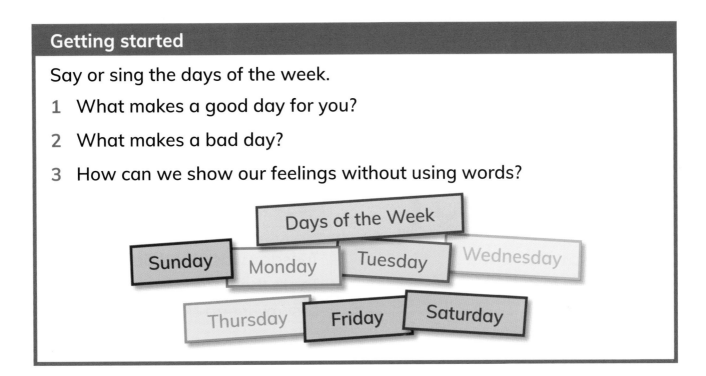

It's a bad day when my friends don't play with me.

It's a good day when we play outside.

1   Listen to and read *Bad Day, Good Day* by Roderick Hunt.
     It is a rhyming story.

     Point to each day of the week as you hear it.

Bad Day, Good Day

Monday was a bad day.

Monday was a bad day.
Clumsy boy-day.
Broke my toy-day.

Tuesday was a sad day.

Tuesday was a sad day.
That's the end-day.
Lost my friend-day.

Wednesday was a tough day.

Wednesday was a tough day.
Lost my kit-day.
Had to sit-day.

Thursday was a late day.

Thursday was a late day.
Had to run-day.
Dropped my bun-day.

Friday was a horrid day.

Friday was a horrid day.
Lip got split-day.
Full of grit-day.

Saturday was an awful day.

Saturday was an awful day.
Mum got mad-day.
Made me sad-day.

Sunday was a fun day.

Sunday was a fun day.
A closing eyes-day.
Big surprise-day…
A Happy Birthday!

Roderick Hunt

How are we doing?

How does joining the words help you to read the rhyme?

2   Write the answers to these questions.

   a   Who is the main character in the rhyme?

   b   What kind of day was Tuesday?

   c   What did she do on Thursday?

   d   How did the character feel on Sunday? Why?

   e   Write a question about the rhyme. Ask someone in your class!

3   Change the underlined words to new words about what kind
    of day it was. Write the new words in your notebook.

Day	Change	Say why
Monday was a <u>bad</u> day	Monday was a happy day.	Went swimming day. Got splashed day.
Tuesday was a <u>sad</u> day.		
Wednesday was a <u>tough</u> day.		
Thursday was a <u>late</u> day.		
Friday was a <u>horrid</u> day.		
Saturday was an <u>awful</u> day.		
Sunday was a <u>fun</u> day.		

4   Use your new words to write your own Bad Day, Good Day rhyme.
    Copy it in neat handwriting in your notebook.

> 6.6 Look back

We are going to...

- **check our writing and look back at our learning.**

Getting started

| Read your rhyme aloud to a partner. |
| Ask: How did it sound? |

| Listen to your partner reading aloud. |
| Tell them how it sounded. |

| Say one thing that was done well. |
| Say one thing you think could have been better. |

1 Use the flow chart from Getting started to check your work with a partner.

How are we doing?

How did you show you were listening well to your partner's rhyme?

How did you show you had read your partner's rhyme carefully?

Reading tip

When you check your writing:

- read it to check meaning first
- then read it to check spelling, capital letters and full stops and if it makes sense.

2 Look back at all the rhymes in this unit.

   a Read, sing or say each one.

   b Use these pictures to help you remember what they were about.

3 Which rhyme or poem did you like:

   a saying or singing?   **b** listening to?

   c reading?   **d** writing?

Say why.

Draw and write your answers.

Look what I can do!

☐ I can listen to and read rhyming poems.

☐ I can explore sounds and rhyming words in poems.

☐ I can answer questions to show my understanding.

☐ I can perform a rhyming poem in a group.

☐ I can plan and write a new rhyme about good and bad days.

☐ I can check my writing and think about my learning in the unit.

Check your progress

Answer the questions below to show what you have learned in this unit.

1 Say what you can do with each of your five senses.

2 Write a word that rhymes with *I* but has a different spelling.

3 Say what kinds of rhyming sounds you like.

4 Write a sentence about a good day.

Projects

Group project: Make an audio bank of poems and rhymes from this unit.

Pair project: Make a simple board game about being sad and happy.

Solo Project: Learn a new poem by heart. Say it to your family or the class.

7 ▷ You'll never believe it!

❯ 7.1 Let's pretend

We are going to...

• talk about places that are real or pretend.

Getting started

1 Talk about the pictures.

2 Are the characters and settings real or pretend?

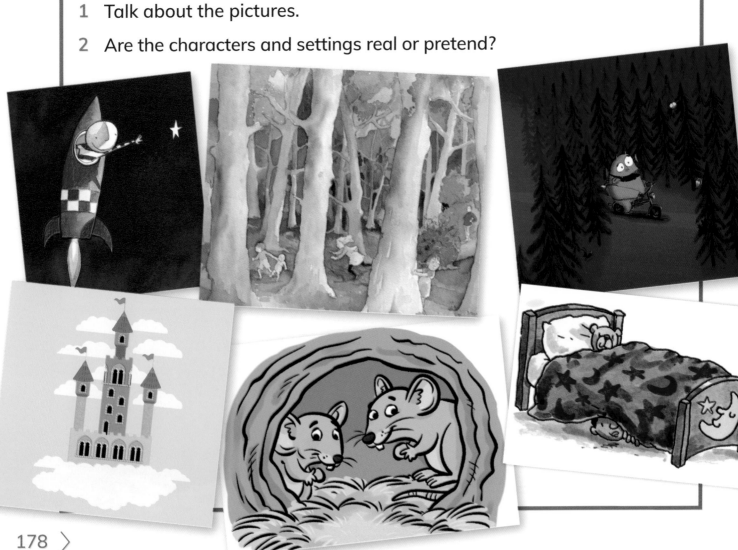

1   Listen to and read *Dragon Land*. Is Dragon Land a real place or a pretend place?

Dragon Land

Five little dragons are flying today over the hills and far away.

'Look at me Mother, look what I can do. I can swoop over the Golden Castle.'

'Look at me Mother, look what I can do. I can zoom over the Enchanted Forest.'

'Look at me Mother, look what I can do. I can soar over the Land of the Giants.'

'Look at me Mother, look what I can do. I can glide over the Marvellous Mountains.'

'But Mother, I can't swoop or zoom. I can't soar or glide.'

'Yes you can, just hop on and ride!'

So Little Dragon number five, climbed on board and felt ALIVE!

Gill Budgell

2 Answer the questions. Write and draw your answers in a list.

a Where do the little dragons fly to?

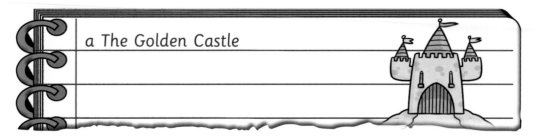

a The Golden Castle

b Which words describe how the dragons fly?

3 In a group, draw a map of a pretend land.

Think of some fun names for each place in the land.

> 7.2 The Grass House

We are going to...

- **listen to a poem about a quiet place and pretend we are there.**

Getting started

1 Are these quiet or noisy places?

Continued

🎧 46 1 Look at the picture. Then listen to *The Grass House* by Shirley Hughes. Do you think this is a real place or a pretend place?

As you listen, point to:

- the seeds
- the pods
- the weeds
- the tiny little flowers.
- the stalks

2   Pretend you are sitting in the grass house.

What you can see, hear, taste, touch and smell?

Write a list in your notebook.

3   Talk about these pictures.
Match the drawings to the photos of the real things.

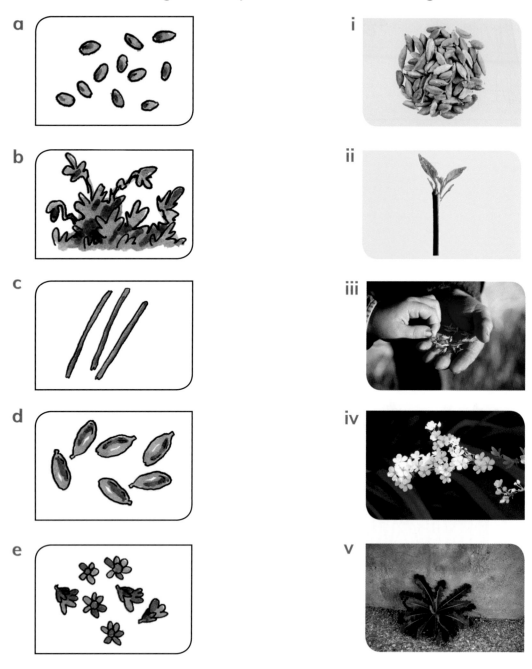

4 Listen again to *The Grass House*.
Write the missing words in your notebook.

> **Writing tip**
>
> Think about the meaning of each word you write.
>
> Then think about the spelling of each word.

a The grass _____ is my private place.

b Nobody can see _____ in _____ grass house.

c Feathery plumes meet over _____ head.

d Only the cat, and _____ busy, hurrying ants know where my grass house is.

> 7.3 How to Catch a Star

We are going to...

- listen to and read a story about trying to do something impossible.

Getting started

1 Look at the pictures.

2 What can you see in the sky?

3 Say and write your answer.

I can see a star in the sky.

I can see a castle in the sky.

1 Listen to and read *How to Catch a Star* by Oliver Jeffers.

   a Listen again.

   b Point to the words and join in where you can.

   c Remember to pause at the full stops.

How to Catch a Star

1 Once there was a boy and the boy loved stars very much.
The boy decided he would try to catch a star.

2 He thought that getting up early in the morning would be best, because then the star would be tired from being up in the sky all night. So, the next day he set out at sunrise. But he could not see a star anywhere.

3 Finally, just before the sun was about to go away, he saw a star. The boy tried to jump up and grab it. But he could not jump high enough. So, very carefully, he climbed to the top of the tallest tree he could find. But the star was still way out of reach.

4 The boy thought he would never catch a star. Just then he noticed something floating in the water.

It was the prettiest star he had ever seen. Just a baby star.

He tried to fish the star out with his hands. But he couldn't reach it.

5 Then he had an idea.

The star might wash up on the shore.

He ran back to the beach …

… and, sure enough, the star washed upon the bright, golden sand.

Oliver Jeffers

2 Talk about when we use *a*, *an* and *the*. Then write one of these words to fill the gaps. Use your notebook.

a Once there was _____ boy and _____ boy loved stars very much.

b _____ boy caught _____ amazing star of his very own.

> ### How are we doing?
>
> The boy in the story had to solve a problem. What do you do to solve problems?

Language focus

We use:

- **the** before singular and plural nouns. *the boy   the boys*

- **a/an** before singular nouns when it does not matter which one we mean. *a star*

We **don't** use:

a/an before plural nouns or names. *a̶ stars*

> 7.4 Checking understanding

We are going to...

- explore the words and sentences in a story to show we understand it.

Getting started

1 Play this star game. How many words can you make beginning or ending with 'star'? Use these pictures to help you:

I am a super*star*!

2 Try again with these words:

sun   moon   boy

1 Read *How to Catch a Star* again.
You will find the story in Session 7.3.

   a Answer *yes* or *no*.

- Did the boy like stars very much?

- Did he catch a star in the morning?

- Did he want to catch the moon?

   b Think of another question beginning
with 'Did ...?' to ask your partner.

2 Match the questions to the answers.

a What did the boy want?	• He climbed to the top of a tree.
b Why did he think it was easy to catch a star in the morning?	• He wanted a star of his very own.
c How did he try to reach the star in the sky?	• He tried to fish it out with his hands.
d How did he try to reach the star in the water?	• He thought the star would be tired.

3 Read the sentences and write them in the correct order.

   a He saw a star in the sea.

   b He tried to catch a star.

   c He saw a star in the sky.

   d The boy wanted a star of his own.

   e He found a star on the beach.

   f The boy had a star of his very own.

› 7.5 Exploring new ideas

We are going to...

- use our imagination to explore new ideas about a story.

Getting started

1 Use the words to sing this song.

Twinkle, twinkle, little star,
How I wonder what you are.
Up above the world so high.
Like a diamond in the sky.
Twinkle, twinkle, little star,
How I wonder what you are.

I know this song. Do you?

1 What would you do with a star of your very own? Write your ideas in your notebook.

2 Talk and write about what **you** would like to try to catch.
How would you catch it?

I would like to catch a _____ because _____

This is how I would do it:

I would...

> **Writing tip**
>
> Remember to use a capital letter for 'I' when you are writing about yourself.

3 Draw the shape of something you want to catch.

a Cut it out.

b Write on it what you would do with the thing you have chosen.

c Read your sentence aloud.

d Hang your shape on something.

> 7.6 We're Going on a Bear Hunt

We are going to...

- listen to and read a story about a difficult journey and a fast return.

Getting started

Pretend you are on a long journey.

1   What will you do when you see these things in your way?

2   Match the descriptions to the photos.

>   a big dark forest
>
>   very tall grass
>
>   a deep cold river

3   What else might get in your way?

1 Listen to and read *We're Going on a Bear Hunt* by Michael Rosen and Helen Oxenbury.

   a Point to each part of the story as you listen.

   b Some parts are repeated. Join in with the repeated words.

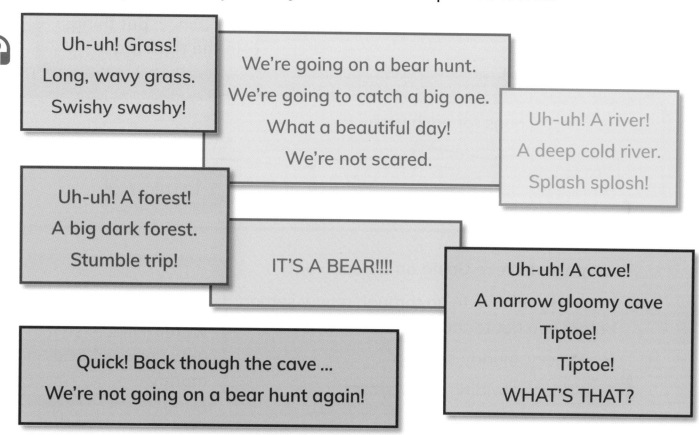

Uh-uh! Grass!
Long, wavy grass.
Swishy swashy!

We're going on a bear hunt.
We're going to catch a big one.
What a beautiful day!
We're not scared.

Uh-uh! A river!
A deep cold river.
Splash splosh!

Uh-uh! A forest!
A big dark forest.
Stumble trip!

IT'S A BEAR!!!!

Uh-uh! A cave!
A narrow gloomy cave
Tiptoe!
Tiptoe!
WHAT'S THAT?

Quick! Back though the cave ...
We're not going on a bear hunt again!

2 Talk about how the story ends.

   a Did you guess the ending?

   b Did you like the ending?

   c Can you think of another ending?

3 Pretend to be the bear. Answer these questions.

   a How did you feel when you saw the people?

   b Do you get many visitors?

> 7.7 Sequencing and retelling

We are going to...

- **sequence** a story and retell it.

Key word

sequence: put things in the right order.

Getting started

1 Make up actions for each verb.

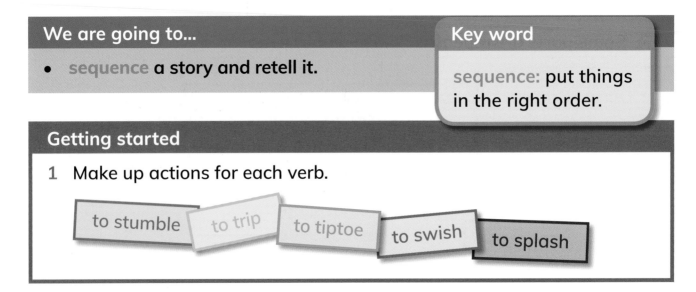

to stumble | to trip | to tiptoe | to swish | to splash

1 Retell part of *We're Going on a Bear Hunt*.

a Pretend you have to go through a new setting before you get to the bear. It might be:

- a sticky, muddy **swamp**

- a bright, swirling snow storm

Glossary

swamp: land where water collects so it gets very wet and muddy.

b Write a sentence for the new setting. Use two joined words to describe how you get through the setting or the sound it makes when you move.

In a sticky muddy swamp I would go sink-squelch!

2 Make a story trail to show the story sequence.

   a Draw your new setting in boxes 4 and 8 in your notebook.

   b Write a sentence for each picture.

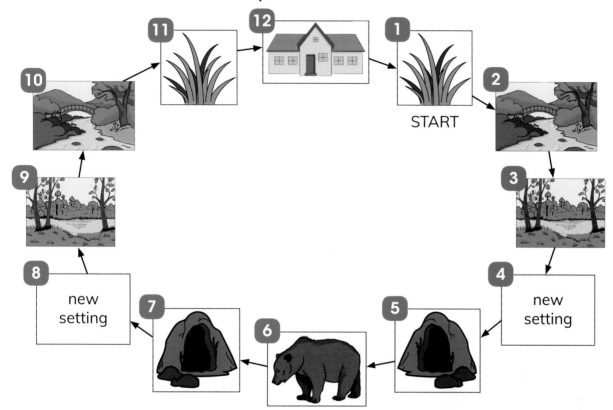

START

4 new setting

8 new setting

3 Use your story trail to retell the story in a group.

Practise telling the story in different ways:

   a with actions

   b with sound effects

   c saying the first part at normal speed and the second part faster, to show you are rushing back home.

How are we doing?

What do you do if you forget how to spell a word?

How are we doing?

Tell your new story to others. What do they think?

4 Work as a class to act the story.
Use some of your own settings and words.

› 7.8 Bedtime for Monsters

We are going to...

- **listen to and read a funny, scary story.**

Getting started

1 Read this story beginning.

> Do you ever wonder if somewhere not too far away there might be

mermaids   dragons   unicorns

2 How could you finish the sentence?

3 How do you feel about these things being near?

1 Listen to and read part 1 of *Bedtime for Monsters* by Ed Vere.

🎧 50 Bedtime for Monsters, Part 1

1 Do you ever wonder if somewhere, not too far
away, there *might* be ... **MONSTERS**?
Do you think that *this* **MONSTER**
might be licking his lips **AND** thinking about
you in an **EATING-YOU-UP** kind of way?

2　He bicycles bumpily through a dark and
　　terrible forest **BUMP BUMPITY BUMP**

3　He crosses the gloopy, schloopy swamp
　　GLOOP GLOOP SCHLOOP

4　He climbs up the cold and snowy mountains,
　　Getting *closer* and *closer* to you, ...
　　You're not **SCARED**, are you?

5　He searches high and low
　　And up and down
　　And in and out
　　All over town ...

6　**DO YOU THINK**
　　He's licking his lips because he wants to
　　GOBBLE YOU UP? **OH NO**,
　　it's much worse than that!
　　THIS monster wants ...

Ed Vere

Speaking tip

Try reading the last part of the story in a different way.
Use a strong or loud voice for the words in capital letters.

2   Say what you think the monster wants to do.
Use the word *and* in your answer.

> 7.9 Comparing story settings

We are going to...

- **check our understanding of the story and compare story settings.**

Getting started

1   Talk to your partner about all the places the monster
from *Bedtime for Monsters* has been to.

2   What other settings can you think of?

1   Read part 2 of *Bedtime for Monsters*. It's the end of the story!

Bedtime for Monsters, Part 2

THIS monster wants ...

a disgustingly big

GOODNIGHT KISS!

Because it's **BEDTIME FOR MONSTERS** everywhere.

a   Did you guess the story ending correctly?

b   Were you scared?

2 Think about the settings in the story.

  a Answer these questions.
  - What is the forest like?
  - What is the swamp like?
  - What are the mountains like?

  b Write a sentence to describe these settings using your own words.

How are we doing?

Would you look for different clues next time?

Reading tip

Look for question marks to help you find questions.

3 Compare story settings for We're Going on a Bear Hunt and Bedtime for Monsters.

  a Copy and finish this chart.

  b Talk about the settings with a partner.
  - Which are the same? • Which are similar? • Which are different?

Setting	1	2	3	4	5
We're Going on a Bear Hunt					house
Bedtime for Monsters	cave				

4 Sort the words into the correct order.

Write the sentences in your notebook.

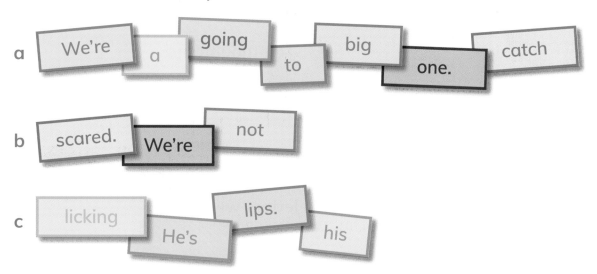

a We're / a / going / to / big / one. / catch

b scared. / We're / not

c licking / He's / lips. / his

> 7.10 Retelling in different ways

We are going to...

- sequence a story and retell it in different ways.

Getting started

Look at these monsters.

1 How can you describe them?

2 How do they make you feel?

1 Sort the pictures into the correct order to tell *Bedtime for Monsters*. Write a sentence for each picture.

a forest

b bedroom

c swamp

d monster cave

e town

f mountains

Writing tip

Think about your handwriting. Which letters will you write in capitals? Which letters will you join?

2 Retell *Bedtime for Monsters* using the pictures and your sentences. Tell it in a scary way.

How are we doing?

How will you make the story sound scary?

> 7.11 Planning and writing

We are going to...

- **plan and write a pretend scary story like one we know.**

Getting started

1 Talk with a partner about this list of story features.

2 Say which features you can see in *Bedtime for Monsters*.

- A main character.

- A journey through different settings.

- Made up or funny words.

I am better at reading words in capital letters.

- Words in capitals or different kinds of letters.

- A surprise ending.

3 Is there anything else you liked about the story?

1   Plan a pretend scary story like *Bedtime for Monsters*.
    Work in pairs.

    a   What is coming to get you? A dinosaur? A giant? A dragon?
        Something else?

    b   Choose four settings your monster travels through to get to you.

    c   Write descriptions for your settings and
        add some funny words for each.

    d   Plan your story ending. Is it funny or scary?

2   Make a storyboard for your story.
    It should look like this.

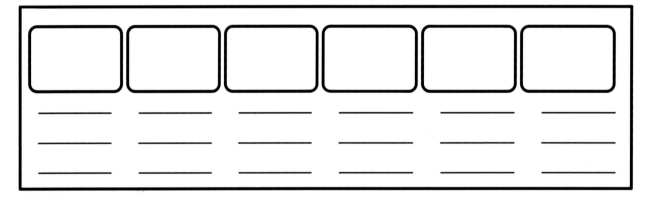

    Draw a picture and write a sentence for each step.
    Use your plans from Activity 1.

3   Stick your storyboard on a big piece of paper. Add:

    • funny repeated words for each setting

    • words in capital letters

    • Do you think ...? questions to make the reader feel a bit scared.

> **Key word**
>
> storyboard: a plan for your story that you draw.

› 7.12 Look back

We are going to...

- **check our writing and look back at our learning.**

Getting started

1   What is the name for the punctuation mark in the speech bubble?

2   When do we use it?

3   Look back to find a full stop in each of the stories in this unit.

It is raining!

1   Check your storyboard writing.

- Check your capital letters.

- Find one word you can write better.

- Did you remember to add full stops at the end of your sentences?

2   Look back at all the stories in this unit.

- Dragon Land

- The Grass House

- How to Catch a Star

- We're Going on a Bear Hunt

- Bedtime for Monsters

Talk about them. Try to remember the characters and the settings.

Which one did you enjoy the most? Why?

3   Say or write one thing you are better at now
    for each of these skills:

reading   writing   spelling   listening   speaking

Look what I can do!

☐   I can explore stories and say what is real and pretend in them.

☐   I can listen for and read words and sentences in stories.

☐   I can join in with stories and retell them.

☐   I can answer questions about stories.

☐   I can plan and write a pretend story.

☐   I can check my writing and talk about my learning in the unit.

Check your progress

Answer the questions below to show what you have learned in this unit.

1   What is a story setting? Write a sentence explaining.

2   Write the rhyming words in this sentence. Which are plural nouns?

    Five little dragons are flying today over the hills and far away.

3   Sort the words to make a sentence:

    read   about   pretend   we   places   stories

4   Fill in the gaps: _____ boy waited and waited to see _____ star.

5   Write one word by joining two smaller words.

6   Finish the sentences:

    a   The scariest story in this unit was ... because ...

    b   The funniest story in this unit was ... because ...

Projects

Group project: Make plans to create a class quiet place where you can enjoy thinking, reading or writing. For example, you could create a simple tent.

Pair project: Build a model to show a pretend world. For example, you could build a simple underwater world.

Solo project: Design and create a pretend place in a box. For example, you could create a box world with unicorns on rainbows and clouds.

8 Finding out

> 8.1 Finding out: what and how?

We are going to...

- think about what we know already and how we can find out more.

Getting started

Talk about how you can find information.

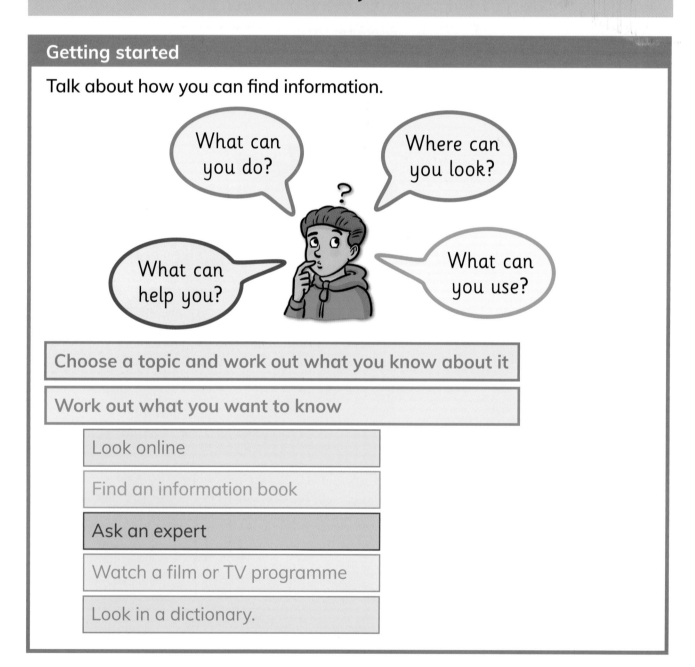

Choose a topic and work out what you know about it

Work out what you want to know

Look online

Find an information book

Ask an expert

Watch a film or TV programme

Look in a dictionary.

1 Talk about these information books.

    a What is each book about?

    b How do the pictures or photos help you to know?

    c What do you think you can find on the back cover?

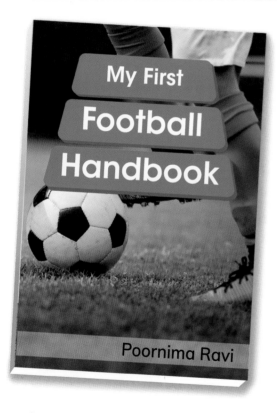

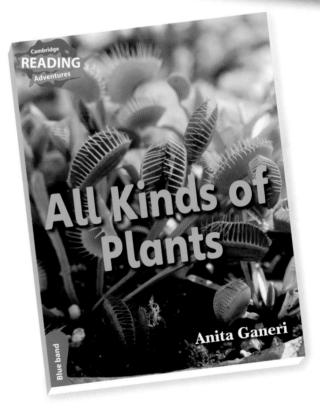

2 In which book can you find out about these things?

Match the pictures to the books in Activity 1.

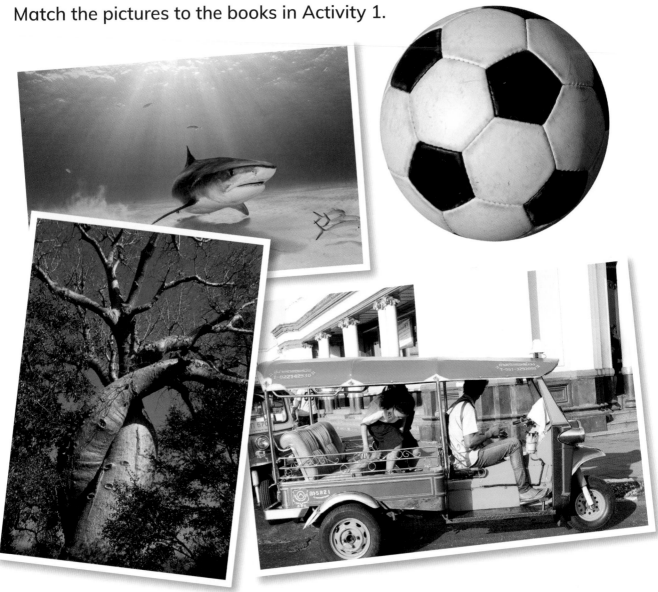

3 What topic would you like to find out more about? Why?

Write your answer. Draw a picture.

> I want to find out more about sea creatures **because** I am interested in whales **and** sharks.

Language focus

Some words help us to join two ideas or two sentences to make one.

and

Some words help us to explain an answer.

because

> 8.2 Exploring a chart

We are going to...

- **explore information in charts.**

Getting started

Work with a partner. Choose an animal.

1 What do you know about this animal?

2 What do you want to find out?

Write three questions about your animal.

Writing tip

Remember to begin your question with a question word.

1   Talk about this chart. Answer the questions with a partner.

   a   What does the chart show you?

   b   Can you name two more animals for each group?

   c   Can you think of any animals that fit into more than one group?

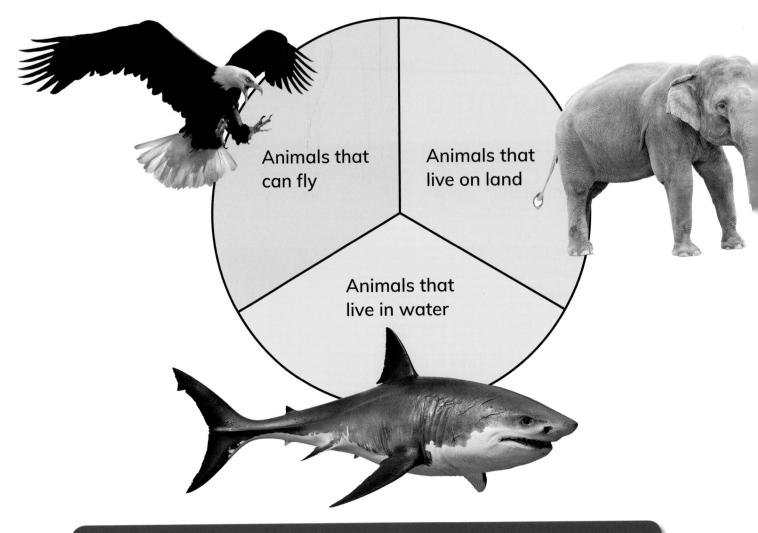

Animals that can fly

Animals that live on land

Animals that live in water

How are we doing?

Have you ever read a chart that has helped you to understand information more clearly?

2 Draw the chart from Activity 1 in your notebook.

   a Sort these animals into the correct groups.

   b Draw and label the animals.

lion

elephant

monkey

crocodile

green turtle

frog

barn owl

shark

seahorse

golden eagle

dragonfly

   c Add more animals to each group.

3 Think of an animal.

   Describe it, but don't say its name.
   Can your partner guess what it is?

My animal lives on land. It is grey. It has very large ears.

> 8.3 Exploring contents information

We are going to...

- **explore contents information.**

Getting started

Talk about this contents page.

1 What is it telling us?

2 What is a contents page for?

3 How does it help us to find information?

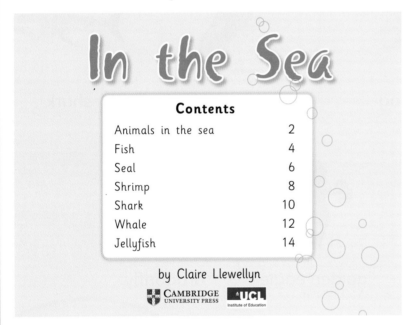

In the Sea

Contents	
Animals in the sea	2
Fish	4
Seal	6
Shrimp	8
Shark	10
Whale	12
Jellyfish	14

by Claire Llewellyn

CAMBRIDGE UNIVERSITY PRESS

UCL Institute of Education

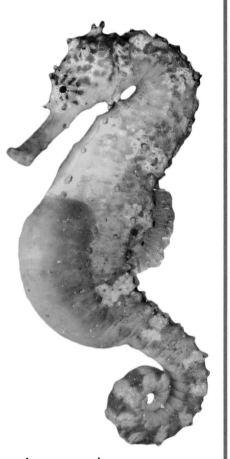

Find some information books with contents pages in your class or school library.

Reading tip

Use phonics to sound out words you do not know how to read.

1   Read and talk about this contents page with a partner.

   a   Which page would you turn to?

   b   Why?

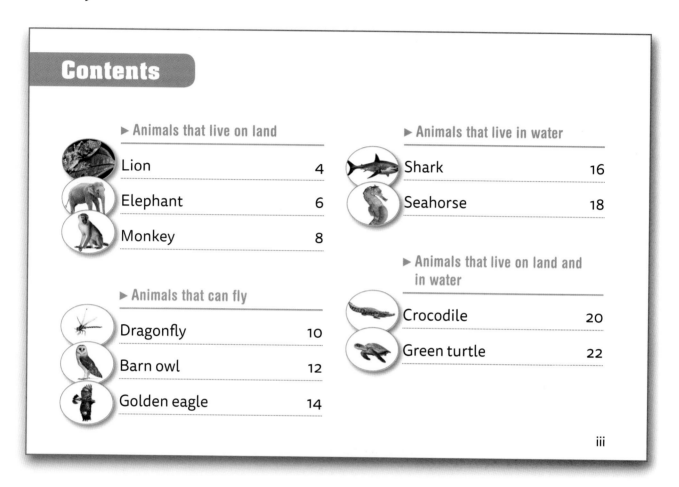

2   Answer these questions about the contents page.
    Write your answers in your notebook.

   a   On which page can you find out about sharks?

   b   In which group are barn owls, dragonflies and golden eagles?

   c   What can you find out about on page 8?

   d   What is different about the animals on pages 20 and 22?

3 Look at a webpage about animals, like this.

   a How can you see what is on the webpage?

   b How is it the same or different from a book contents page?

How are we doing?

How do you prefer to find out about things? Why?

› 8.4 Writing a contents page

We are going to...

- **plan and write a contents page.**

Getting started

Find a book.

Ask a partner to point to: the outside front cover | the inside back cover

a picture | a contents page | the author's name

1   Look again at this contents page.

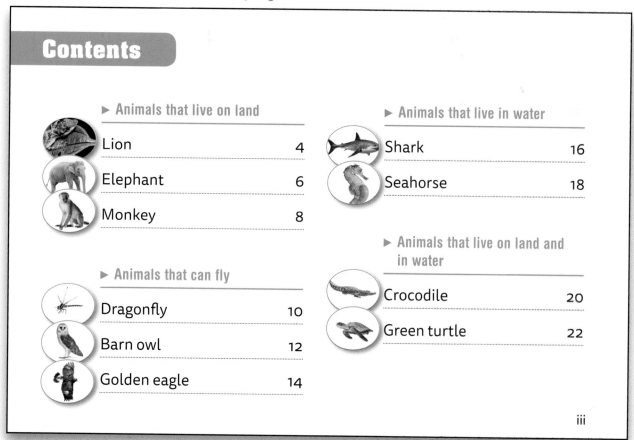

Contents

▶ **Animals that live on land**

Lion 4

Elephant 6

Monkey 8

▶ **Animals that can fly**

Dragonfly 10

Barn owl 12

Golden eagle 14

▶ **Animals that live in water**

Shark 16

Seahorse 18

▶ **Animals that live on land and in water**

Crocodile 20

Green turtle 22

iii

Choose a topic for your own contents page.

Use these ideas to help you:

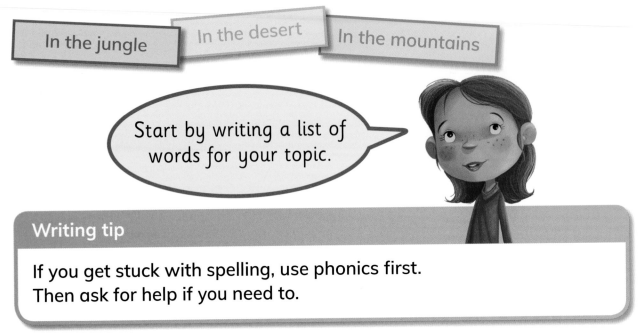

In the jungle   In the desert   In the mountains

Start by writing a list of words for your topic.

Writing tip

If you get stuck with spelling, use phonics first.
Then ask for help if you need to.

2   Write and draw your contents page.

Use the contents page in Activity 1 to help you.

Writing tip

- Write the topic title: In the
- Write the word Contents.
- Draw or write what is in your book in a list.
- Add page numbers (just pretend). Check you write them correctly.
- Add your name as the author.

3   Now design your book cover.

   a   How will you make it look fun to read?

   b   Fix the cover to the contents page.

> 8.5 Exploring pictures and captions

We are going to...

- explore pictures and captions in information books.

Getting started

Talk about drawings and photos. Which do you prefer and why?

1 Listen to the captions about crabs.
Point to the correct photo.

a

b

c

d

2 Read these captions aloud with a partner.

a Copy the captions into your notebook.

b Draw pictures for each.

A giraffe eats leaves from the tops of trees.

A butterfly lands on a flower.

Deep under the sea, a shark swims past a jelly fish.

3 Write captions for these photos in your notebook.

Use these words to help you:

panda

monkeys

penguins

bear

Writing tip

Remember to use capital letters and full stops for your sentences.

› 8.6 Exploring topic words

We are going to...

- **explore topic words.**

Getting started

Talk about your **diet.**

Match the picture to the label.

Glossary

diet: food we eat.

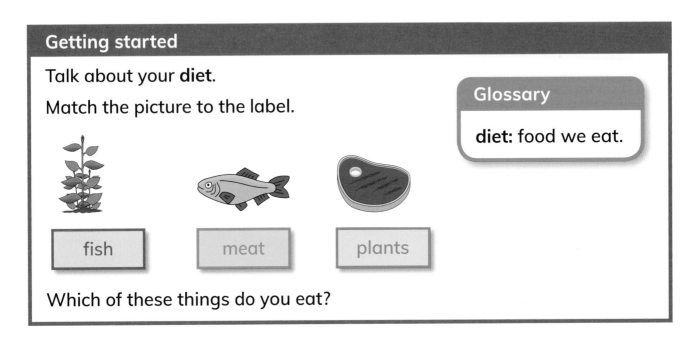

| fish | meat | plants |

Which of these things do you eat?

1   Listen to and read these three sentences about the diet of these baby animals.

Some baby animals only eat meat or fish.

Other animal babies only eat plants.

Many animal babies like to eat meat and plants!

2 Answer these questions in your notebook. Write sentences.

  a What diet do baby tigers eat?

  b What diet do baby elephants eat?

  c What diet do baby bears eat?

Now write a sentence about the diet of another animal.

3 Look at these **habitats**. Match each picture to the correct habitat label.

| mountains | rainforests | seas | ice lands | deserts |

Draw and write the habitats in your notebook.

Reading tip

Use your phonics to sound out parts of these words to help you read them.

Glossary

habitat: where an animal lives.

Writing tip

Topic words are special words about a topic. They are interesting and can help us in our writing.

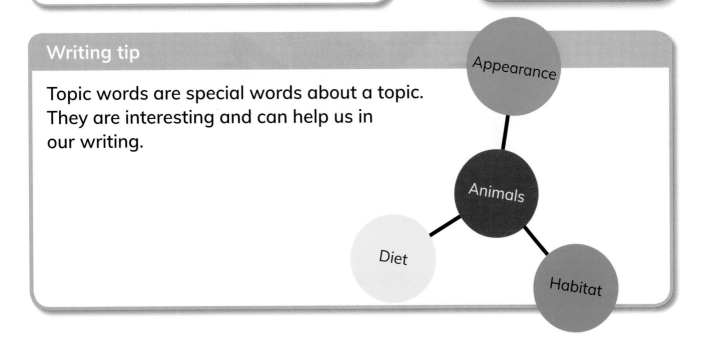

Appearance

Animals

Diet

Habitat

> 8.7 Exploring a glossary

We are going to...

- **explore how to use a glossary.**

Getting started

Make a topic word-chain.

One person says a topic. Each person must add a topic word linked to it.

Shells! Tortoise! Crab! Hard!

1 Talk about and read the labels on this photo.

claw stalk eye leg shell

a Does the photo help you to understand the topic words about crabs? How?

b In your notebook, draw a crab or another animal with a shell. Label it.

2 Listen to and read this report about barn owls.

   a Which topic words do you know?

   b Which words are difficult to understand?

Barn owls

Habitat

Diet

Mother barn owls lay their eggs in holes in trees or in old buildings such as barns. They lay up to seven eggs.

   When the **owlets** are born they eat a lot of food. The parents hunt for mice, frogs and insects to feed them.

   When the owlets **hatch** they have white **down**. After 60 days they have feathers.

mother barn own   owlet

3 Find the words with **brown** letters in the report. Read the **glossary** to check their meaning.

Glossary

owlets: baby owl.

hatch: how a baby bird cracks out of its egg.

down: soft, first feathers of a baby bird.

> 8.8 Exploring a dictionary

We are going to...

- **explore a dictionary.**

Getting started

Write the alphabet. Write a number below each letter.

A B C D E F G H I J K L M N O P Q R S T U V W X Y Z
1 2 3 4 5 6 7 8 9 10 11 12 13 14 15 16 17 18 19 20 21 22 23 24 25 26

Play a game. Ask questions about the 26 letters of the alphabet.

What is the first letter of the alphabet?

What is letter number 26?

What is letter number 5?

1 Talk about this page from a dictionary.

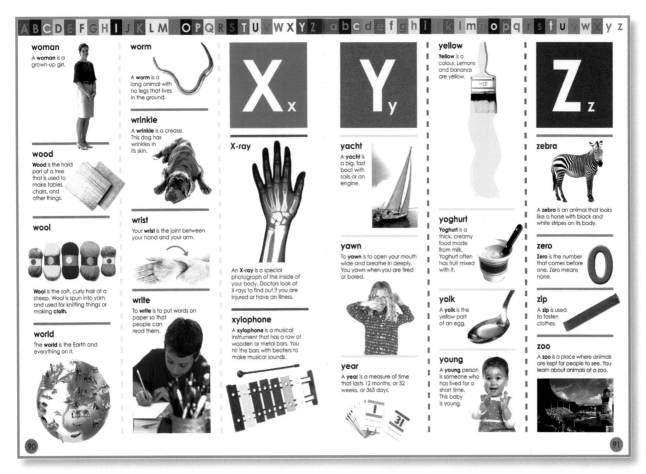

Look for examples of a, an or the.

2 Answer these questions.
Reread the word meanings from the dictionary page.

a What is a worm?

b What is a yolk?

c What is a zebra?

d What is this?

Key word

dictionary: a list of words in A–Z alphabetical order. It explains the meaning of words. It may show pictures and photos too.

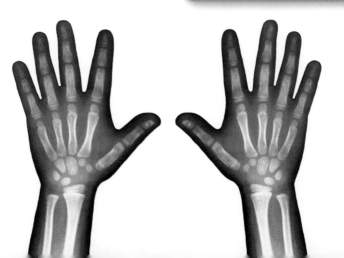

3 Write your own dictionary page.

a Choose a letter. Write the upper case letter and the lower case letter in your notebook.

b Write three words that begin with the letter.

c Write what the words mean and draw pictures for each.

Writing tip

Remember to check your use of a, *an* or *the*.

> ## 8.9 Exploring a fact file

We are going to...

- **talk, read about and write an animal fact file.**

Getting started

Talk about how a duck, an eagle and a panda are similar to a penguin.

an eagle

a duck

a panda

Reading tip

Use your phonics to read the animal names.

1 Listen to and read this fact file about the Emperor Penguin.

Point to the labelled parts of the penguin as you read or hear them.

Habitat

Diet

Emperor Penguins

Emperor penguins are the largest kind of penguin. They can be 130 cm tall.

They live in Antarctica in **colonies**.

They eat fish.

black, white and yellow feathers

long, hooked beak

webbed feet

thick layers of fat

sharp claws

short wings

brood pouch

Fun facts
- They have strong claws for gripping the ice.
- They have webbed feet for fast swimming.
- They have a **brood pouch** for keeping their chicks safe and warm.
- They cannot fly.

Glossary

colonies: a big group.

brood pouch: a pocket or flap of skin to protect baby animals.

Now read the text aloud with a partner.

2 Read these facts about the Emperor penguin. Say true or false.

  a They are the largest kind of penguin.

  b Their habitat is very warm.

  c They fly fast.

  d They are good swimmers.

  e They have feet like ducks.

3 Write a fact file for an animal you know about.

  a Draw your animal.

  b Label its features.

  c Write some fun facts about it.

Reading tip

If you need help to read the words, ask a partner.

> 8.10 Exploring a report

We are going to...

- talk about and read a report about an animal.

Getting started

Talk about and name these animals.

They all live in ice lands.

- What does an ice land habitat look like?
- Why are these animals mainly white?

1 Listen to and read this report about harp seals.

When you have finished listening, talk with a partner about a fact you remember.

Harp seal

The name for a baby seal is pup. They are born on ice. The mother seal feeds her pups on milk for about 12 days. She then swims away.

The pups have white fur for about two weeks. The white fur helps the pups to keep safe.

After that, dark hair grows under their white fur and they turn grey. The pups can then swim off to find fish to eat.

Habitat

Diet

Did you know?
Seals can stay under the water for up to 30 minutes.

white fur

seal pup

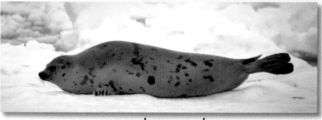

mother seal

Language focus

Common words are words that we have to read a lot.

the for a is they are on

How are we doing?

Which common words can you now read well? Which common words do you find difficult to read?

2 Answer these questions in your notebook.

   a What is the name of a baby seal?

   b How long do the pups keep their white fur?

   c What do harp seals eat?

   d Where do harp seals live?

   e Choose two words to explain in a glossary.

3 Which features can you find in the Harp Seal report? Write a list in your notebook.

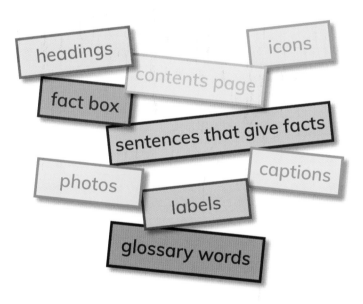

headings

icons

contents page

fact box

sentences that give facts

photos

captions

labels

glossary words

Remember, a glossary explains difficult words using easier words.

> 8.11 Planning and writing a report

We are going to...

- **talk about, plan and write a report.**

Getting started

Look at this chart with a partner. Which features do reports have?

Does it have ...	Yes or no?
a story?	
a heading?	
facts?	
a glossary?	
a list of things you need?	
pictures or photos with captions?	

Is there anything else a report could have?

1   Write a chart like the one in Getting started to show the features of the Harp Seal report in Session 8.10.

Keep your chart safe so you can use it to check your own report writing.

You can use the list you wrote in Activity 3 in Session 8.10

2 Plan your own report.

   a Choose an animal.

   b Think of some facts about your animal.
      Do you need to find out more facts?

   c Think about how you will show your animal facts.

Did you know?   Fun facts   Star facts

   d Where will you find pictures or photos?

3 Write your report.

   a Use your features chart and planning notes to help you.

   b Use this layout guide to help you.

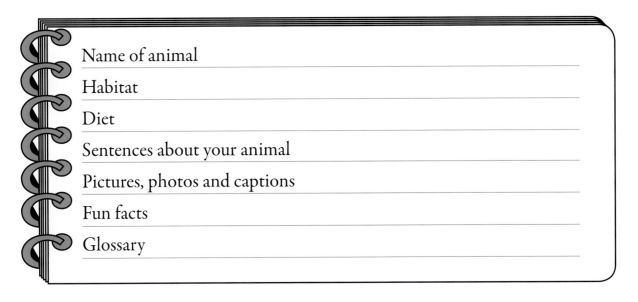

Name of animal

Habitat

Diet

Sentences about your animal

Pictures, photos and captions

Fun facts

Glossary

〉 8.12 Look back

We are going to...

- **check our writing and look back at our learning.**

Getting started

How can we check our writing?

What will we need to check?

1 Check your writing.

 a Look at how you set out your report in Session 8.11.

 b Look at the features checklist you made.

 c Did you use all the features? Why?

> Did you remember to add fun facts to your report?

How are we doing?

Share your report. What do others think of it?

2 Look back at all the different ways of finding information in this unit.

   a Talk about them with a partner.

   b Try to remember the correct name for each one.

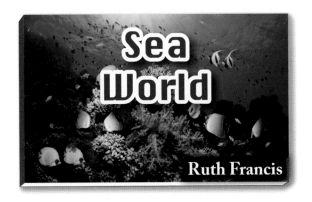

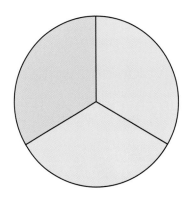

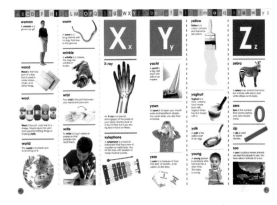

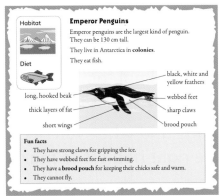

3 Say or write one thing you learned to help with these skills:

reading   writing   spelling   listening   speaking

Look what I can do!

☐ I can work out what I know and what I want to find out about.

☐ I can explore and use topic words.

☐ I can use book covers and contents pages to find information.

☐ I can use pictures and photos to help me find information.

☐ I can plan and write a fact file and a report.

☐ I can check my writing and talk about my learning in the unit.

Check your progress

Answer the questions below to show what you have learned in this unit.

1 What can you use to help you to understand new words?

2 What does a contents page tell you?

3 Write a caption for this photograph.

4 Say the alphabet.

5 What is another word for *home*?

6 What is the difference between a fact file and a report?

Projects

Group project: Make an A–Z washing line of animal facts. Draw a triangle for each letter of the alphabet and write a fact for each letter.

Pair project: List what you know about bugs and what you need to find out. Work out what you need to create the right habitat to make the bugs feel welcome!

Solo project: Find an information book that you find really interesting. Design a bookmark for it. Write three words to say what you can learn from the book. Put it in the book for someone to find.

9 All kinds of weather

> ## 9.1 Whatever the weather

We are going to...

- **explore poems about weather.**

Getting started

Look at the pictures. What do they mean?

Use these words to help you.

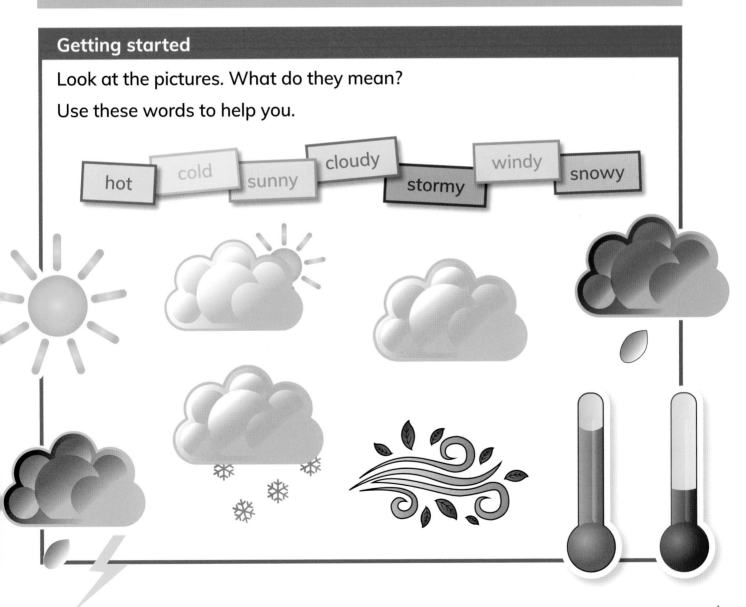

hot   cold   sunny   cloudy   stormy   windy   snowy

What is the weather like today where you live?

Language focus

We can use **and**

- to join two words: hot   cold   hot **and** cold
- to join two sentences: It's hot today. It's sunny today.
  It's hot **and** sunny today.

1   Read these poems. What are they about?

a   Rain on the green grass
And rain on the tree
And rain on the house top
But not on me!

b   Sun up
Sun hat
Sun glasses
Lie flat.
Sun cream
Sun shine
Sun down
Sleep time.

c   The wind blows the clouds
The wind blows me
Where does the wind go?
Can you tell me?

d   I hear thunder
I hear thunder
Can you too? Can you too?
Pitter-patter raindrops
Pitter-patter raindrops
I'm wet through
So are you!

2 Work in a group to say or sing one poem out loud.

Speaking tip

- Open your mouth wide.
- Speak or sing with a loud clear voice.

3 Read the poem again.

Change the words by filling the gaps to write your own poem. Write your poem in your notebook.

You don't need to use rhyming words.

Rain on the _____

And rain on the sea

And rain on the _____

But not on me!

Rain on the _____

And rain on you

Rain on the _____

And on me too!

〉 9.2 Words in shapes

We are going to...

- **talk about, read and write a weather shape poem.**

Getting started

Listen to *Sunshine*

1   Write the letters you hear.

2   Say what words the letters spell.

3   Listen again. Write two words that rhyme.

How are we doing?

In *Sunshine*, we heard two words: **ultra** and **hazy**.
Do you know what they mean?

ultra means very   **hazy** means not clear

1   Look at *Rainbow* by Gill Rujaro Magwenzi.

How do you think you should read this poem?

Read the poem.

Reading tip

Read down for *rain*, across for SUN and round for *rainbow*.

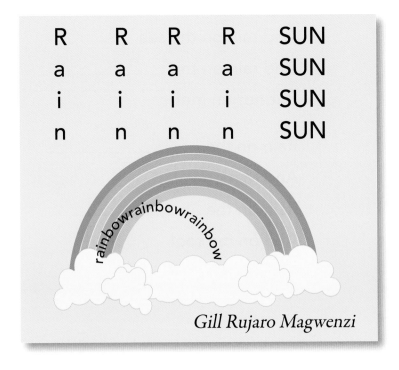

Gill Rujaro Magwenzi

2   Read the sentences about *Rainbow*. Say *true* or *false*.

    a   The letters in the word *rain* are falling like rain.

    b   The word *rainbow* is shaped like a cloud.

    c   The poem is the shape of the thing it is describing.

    d   The word *sun* is in capitals because the poem is about the sun.

3   Write these words in a way that shows their meaning.

4   Write a shape poem about weather.

    a   Draw a weather shape.

    b   Write a list of words that match the weather you have chosen.

    c   Write weather words, phrases or sentences inside your shape.

Writing tip

Think carefully about where to write your letters and words. Your poem doesn't have to rhyme, but your words must be linked to the weather shape you have chosen.

> 9.3 Describing weather

We are going to...

- talk, read about and write a weather poem.

Getting started

Talk about snow and ice.

Use these words to help you:

cold   icy   sparkly   white   deep   soft

1   Read *How Do I Describe the Snow* by Bashabi Fraser.
    What does this poem tell you about snow?

How Do I Describe the Snow?

My cousins have asked me

To describe the snow

But I really don't know

How to tell them how

Softly it falls

How gently it fills

Our garden. How wet

It feels after it settles

On my shoulders

How freshly it crunches

Under my heels

How quickly it slides

Down a slippery bank

How thickly it lies

In the school yard

How easily it rolls

Into a ball

How swiftly it

Can shoot away

From my hand

And smash

Against my friend's back

To melt into powder

And be lost in the snow

On the playground!

Bashabi Fraser

2   Talk about these questions in a group.
    Write your answers together.

    a   Where do you think the cousins live?

    b   Why doesn't the poet know how to describe
        snow for her cousins?

    c   How does she make snow sound?

3   Change the words by filling the gaps to write your own poem
about the weather. Write your poem in your notebook.

My cousins have asked me

To describe the _____ But I really don't know

How to tell them how _____ly it _____

How _____ it looks How _____ it feels.

> 9.4 Weather is like a ...

We are going to...

- explore ideas and words about what weather is like.

Getting started

Look at these weather pictures. Talk about what the weather looks like.

How are we doing?

What helps you to use your imagination?

1 Listen to *Thunder* by Romesh Gunesekera and *Lightning* by Gill Budgell.

   a What is thunder like?

   b What is lightning like?

   c Read the poems aloud.

Thunder

is nothing more
than the roar
of an elephant's snore

           Romesh Gunesekera

Lightning

is nothing more
than the electric hiss
of a snake's kiss

      Gill Budgell

2   Listen to Storm by a Year 3 student.
    Then answer these questions about
    the poem.

    a   What does it tell us to imagine?

    b   What do you imagine a storm to be?

3   Look at the pictures in Getting started.

    Write a caption for each one in your notebook.

    Use the chart to help you.

	sea			crashes.
	lightning			flashes.
Imagine the		is a _____	when it	
	sun			shines.
	tornado			twists.

Language focus

We begin a sentence with a capital letter and
end it with a full stop.

> 9.5 Planning and writing an adventure poem

We are going to...

- plan and write an adventure poem.

Getting started

Talk about how you like to play in different weather.

These children are pretending.

1 Give each picture a title.

2 Say a sentence for each picture.

One sunny day ...   *One snowy day ...*   *One rainy day ...*

1   Listen to and read *One Wet Day* by Richard Edwards.

   a   Point to the names of the children as you hear them.

   b   What is Jackie pretending to be?

   c   What is Zuleika pretending to be?

One Wet Day

Jackie put her red shoes on

And her red coat

And her red woolly hat

And went out of the back door
   into the garden

To pick a strawberry.

Zuleika put one black and one
   orange shoe on

And her gold sash,

Stuck a feather in her hair

And went out of the back door
   into the rain forest

To track panthers.

Richard Edwards

2 Compare what Jackie and Zuleika do on the wet day.

a Copy and fill in a chart like this.

Name	Put on	Went	Where to?	Why?
Jackie		*out of the back door*		
Zuleika				

b Say which would you choose to do.

c Say why.

3 Add a line to the chart in Activity 2.

a Write what you would put on, where you would go to and why.

b Write your own poem using the ideas.

c Draw what you are pretending to be.

I put on _____ and _____

And my _____

Stuck a _____

And went out of the back door into the _____

To _____ .

Use these sentences to help you fill the gaps with your own ideas.

> 9.6 Look back

We are going to...

- check our writing and look back at our learning.

Getting started

We use some words more than others.

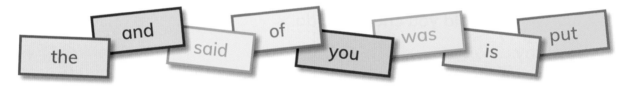

1 Look at some of your writing from this unit.

2 Write a list of words you use a lot.

3 Do you always spell them correctly?

1 Check your writing.

Read your poem from Session 9.5 quietly to yourself.
Then read it out loud.

How are we doing?

What did you think of your poem?

What could you improve?

What helped you most: reading quietly to yourself or reading out loud? Why?

2 Look back at the poems in this unit.

   a Say what they are about.

   b Write the title of each poem and draw a matching weather picture.

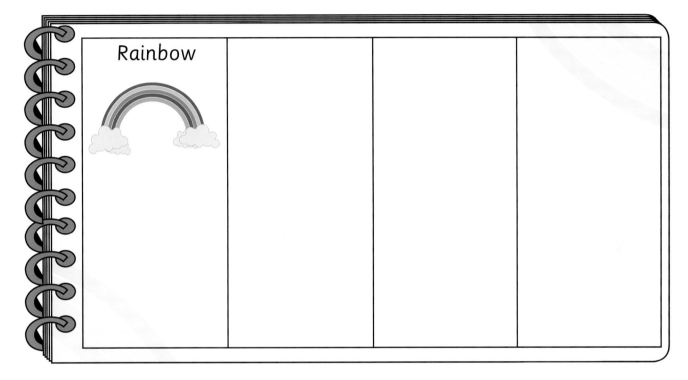

3 Read your chart.

   a Say which poem you liked best and why.

   b Draw and write your answers.

Look what I can do!

☐ I can explore poems about weather.

☐ I can talk about, read and write a weather shape poem.

☐ I can write a poem about weather.

☐ I can explore words and ideas about what weather is like.

☐ I can plan and write a new adventure poem.

☐ I can check my writing and talk about my learning in the unit.

Check your progress

Answer the questions below to show what you have learned in this unit.

1   What types of weather do you know?

2   Write some sunshine words in a sunshine way.

3   Write a sentence to describe a type of weather.
    Ask someone to guess what you are describing.

4   What do you think a storm is like?

Projects

Group project: Set up an imagination corner so that you can pretend to go anywhere and be anything on a rainy day or a day that is too hot to play outside.

Pair project: Choose a new theme and find three poems to match it.

Solo project: Find a new weather poem and write it in a shape that matches.

> Toolkit

Speaking with others

> Hello. My name is Anya.
> What is your name?
> I am six. How old are you?
> I live in the country.
> Where do you live?

> Can I help you, please?
> Can you help me, please?
> Let's take it in turns. It's your turn now!

Happy Birthday!

> Hello. How are you today?
> It's my birthday today.
> When is your birthday?
> Bye! See you soon.

Story characters

These are people or animals in a story.

Story settings

These are places where stories take place.

Information texts

These can:

- **tell us about things people have done**

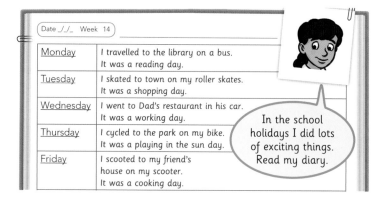

Date _/_/_ Week 14	
Monday	I travelled to the library on a bus. It was a reading day.
Tuesday	I skated to town on my roller skates. It was a shopping day.
Wednesday	I went to Dad's restaurant in his car. It was a working day.
Thursday	I cycled to the park on my bike. It was a playing in the sun day.
Friday	I scooted to my friend's house on my scooter. It was a cooking day.

In the school holidays I did lots of exciting things. Read my diary.

- **tell us how to do things**

Recipe:

How to make chocolate-chip muffins

What to do:

1. Put in the flour.
2. Put in the baking powder. Mix.
3. Put in the sugar.
4. Put in the choc chips. Mix.
5. Put in the eggs. Mix.
6. Put in the milk. Mix.
7. Bake the muffins in the oven.

- **help us to find out about things.**

In the Sea

Contents

by Claire Llewellyn

CAMBRIDGE UNIVERSITY PRESS UCL Institute of Education

Poems

These can:

- have rhythm
- have rhyme
- be about the same topic.

Finger trace and copy the days of the week words.

Monday	**Fri**day
Tuesday	**Satur**day
Wednesday	**Sun**day
Thursday	

Finger trace and copy the colour words.

red	**brown**
yellow	**pink**
green	**purple**
blue	orange
white	grey
black	

Finger trace and copy the numbers, number words and patterns.

1 /
one

2 --
two

3 |||
three

4 ////
four

5 >>>>>
five

6 w w
six

7 >>> > >>>
seven

8 cccc cccc
eight

9 www www www
nine

10 OOOO OOOO
ten

Letters and sounds

Remember that your read and write English this way, → left to right.

Say the letters, say the letter sounds.

Finger trace and copy the letters in your notebook

s, a, t, n, i, p, o, g, d, m, c, k, r, e, u, h, b, l, f, j, v, w, y, z

ll, ff, ss, zz

ck, ng, nk, th, sh, ch

x, qu

ai, ee , igh, oa, oo

ar, or, ir, er, ow, oi, ear, air

Read the words in the charts.

Finger trace and copy the words in your notebook.

Word	Rhyming words with the same end spelling
hat	bat, cat, mat, rat
ten	den, hen, men, pen
kit	bit, fit, hit, sit
fog	dog, hog, jog, log
bug	hug, jug, mug, rug
day	say, pay, way
jeep	deep, keep, weep
light	night, right, sight
coat	boat, goat, moat
too	boo, coo, moo
book	cook, look, hook

Word	Words with the same vowel sound but a different spelling
r**ai**n	day
b**ee**	me, tea
h**igh**	lie, my, sky, bye
c**oa**t	no, low, toe
b**oo**	blew, two, who
f**air**	pear, share, where
g**ir**l	curl

Common words

Read the words in the charts.

Finger trace and copy the words in your notebook.

a, an, at, if, in, is, it, off, on, can, dad, had, back, and, get, big, him, not, got, up, mum, but, put

will, that, this, then, them, with, see, for, now, down, look, too

of, his, as, the, to, I, no, go, into

he, she, we, me, be, was, you, they, all, are, my, her

The Alphabet

Say the alphabet. Finger trace each letter and copy into your notebook.

abcdefghijk
lmnopqrstuv
wxyz

ABCDEFGHI
JKLMNOPQR
STUVWXYZ

Punctuation

Read this sentence. Finger trace the letters and copy into your notebook. Check the punctuation is correct.

capital letter

This is the end of the book.

full stop

Key words

› Acknowledgements

The authors and publishers acknowledge the following sources of copyright material and are grateful for the permissions granted. While every effort has been made, it has not always been possible to identify the sources of all the material used, or to trace all copyright holders. If any omissions are brought to our notice, we will be happy to include the appropriate acknowledgements on reprinting.

Unit 1: Illustrations and story adapted from *It's much too early!* by Ian Whybrow (Cambridge Reading Adventures). Published by Cambridge University Press 2016. Story used by permission of Ian Whybrow; Excerpts from *Don't Spill the Milk* by Stephen Davies, illustrated by Christopher Corr reproduced by the permission of Andersen Press; Extracts and illustrations from *Hide and Seek* by Lynne Rickards, (Cambridge Reading Adventures). Published by Cambridge University Press 2016; Excerpt from *THE PARK IN THE DARK* by Martin Waddell, Text © 1989 Martin Waddell, Reproduced by permission of Walker Books Ltd, London SE11 5HJ www.walker.co.uk **Unit 2**: Extracts and illustrations from *My First Train Trip* by Lynne Rickards, (Cambridge Reading Adventures). Published by Cambridge University Press 2016; Excerpt from *A Week in the Holidays* by Gill Budgell published by Cambridge University Press; Excerpts and illustrations from *Cloud Nine* written by Gill Budgell reproduced by permission of Franklin Watts, an imprint of Hachette Children's Books; **Unit 3:** *One, Two, Buckle my Shoe* by Gill Budgell and Kate Ruttle, reproduced by permission of Cambridge University Press; Excerpts from *I got the Rhythm* by Schofield Morrison copyright 2014, reproduced by permission of Bloomsbury Publishing Inc; Adapted extract and illustrations from *Red is a Dragon* copyright 2001 by Roseanne Thong, Used with permission of Chronicle Books LLC, San Francisco; **Unit 4:** Excerpts from *The Runaway Chapati; A Chapati; Run, Run; Stop, Come Back!* by Gill Budgell and Kate Ruttle reproduced by permission of Cambridge University Press with Illustrations by Stephen Waterhouse; Adapted extract from *The Big Pancake* by Susan Gates & Alan Rogers, Cambridge Reading Adventures, Cambridge University Press; Adapted extract from *One Day in the Eucalyptus, Eucalyptus Tree* by Daniel Bernstrom Illustrated By Brendan Wenzel. Text Copyright 2016 by Daniel Bernstrom Illustrations Copyright 2016 by Brendan Wenzel. Reproduced by permission of HarperCollins Publishers; **Unit 5:** Excerpt from *Make Colours* by Gill Budgell, by of Cambridge University Press, photographs Graham Portlock; Excerpt from *More-Igami* by Dori Kleber and illustrated by G. Brian Karas Reproduced by permission of Walker Books Ltd, London SE11 5HJ www.walker.co.uk, Text© 2016 Dori Kleber, Illustrations © G. Brian Karas; **Unit 6:** Excerpt from 'Sand in your fingernails' by John Foster, published in *Poems for the Very Young* (Kingfisher Books), used by kind permission of the author; 'Sand' and 'Sick' © 1988 Shirley Hughes from *OUT AND ABOUT* by Shirley Hughes Reproduced by permission of Walker Books Ltd; Excerpt from 'Laughing Time' from *Laughing Time: Collected Nonsense* by William Jay Smith, illustrated by Fernando Krahn. Copyright 1990 by William Jay Smith. Reprinted by permission of Farrar, Straus and Giroux Books for Young Readers and the Estate of William Jay Smith; Excerpt from *Bad Day, Good Day* by Roderick Hunt, illustrated by Jan Lewis , published by Oxford University Press; **Unit 7:** 'The Grass House' © 1988 Shirley Hughes From OUT AND ABOUT by Shirley Hughes Reproduced by permission of Walker Books Ltd; Excerpts and illustrations from *How to Catch a Star* by